NIETZSCHE

within your grasp™

By Shelley O'Hara

WILEY

Wiley Publishing, Inc.

Nietzsche Within Your Grasp™

Copyright © 2004 Wiley, Hoboken, NJ

Published by:

Wiley Publishing, Inc.

111 River Street

Hoboken, NJ 07030-5774

www.wiley.com

Published simultaneously in Canada

Cataloguing-in-Publication Data available from the Library of Congress.

Library of Congress Catalogue Card No.: 2004101612

ISBN: 0-7645-5975-3

1Q/QR/QW/QU/IN

Manufactured in the United States of America

10 9 8 7 6 5 4 3 2

Table of Contents

Acknowledgments

A bouquet of thanks to Cindy Kitchel for suggesting me for this project. A round of applause and cheers to Greg Tubach, Acquisitions Editor; Elizabeth Kuball, Project Editor Extraordinaire; and Dave Stout, Technical Editor and Philosophy Scholar.

1 Nietzsche's Life

One must still have chaos in oneself to be able to give birth to a dancing star.
—Nietzsche, *Thus Spoke Zarathustra*

Much has been written about Friedrich Nietzsche. Although he was not influential during his lifetime, his work has influenced and continues to influence many philosophers, writers, artists, painters, psychologists, sociologists, and revolutionaries. Although his influence in non-English-speaking continental Europe was much greater than in the rest of Western thought, Nietzsche is still one of the most influential, notorious, and most cited philosophers today.

A lot of what seems to be common knowledge about Nietzsche is myth. His work has been misinterpreted to support many controversial views, but it is the misuse of his writing, taken out of context. He was not a Nazi or an anti-Semite or a supporter of Hitler. This chapter uncovers how some of these beliefs came about.

Some of the other notorious things about Nietzsche *are* true. He did say, infamously, "God is dead." He was an atheist, and he did suffer a mental breakdown and was committed to an asylum for much of the last part of his life. This chapter provides a timeline for Nietzsche's work and some key events so that you can get a perspective of his life. Start by looking at his upbringing, influences, education, and key events, as covered here.

Early Education

Friedrich Nietzsche was born in Roecken, Prussia, on October 15, 1844, to Karl Ludwig and Franziska Nietzsche. His father was a Lutheran pastor, as was his father before him. Karl died at the age of 35, when Friedrich was only 4 years old. Friedrich's younger brother, Joseph, died shortly after the death of his father, and Friedrich was raised by his grandmother, mother, two paternal aunts, and sister, Elisabeth. They doted on young "Fritz," who showed early promise as a poet, musician, and scholar.

Much has been said about the influence of being raised in such a feminine environment, but Nietzsche's writing about women does not enable the reader to draw one consistent conclusion. In *Thus Spoke Zarathustra,* Nietzsche writes, "The true man wants two things: danger and play. For that reason he wants woman, as the most dangerous plaything." In *The Anti-Christ,* he writes, "Woman was God's second mistake." But then he says, "Yes, life is a woman!" in *The Gay Science.* Nietzsche neither married nor had any substantial love interest in his life.

In 1850, the family moved to Naumburg, and Nietzsche attended a private preparatory school. Nietzsche also began piano lessons and started creating his own musical compositions and writing poems.

In 1858, Nietzsche received a scholarship to a leading Protestant boarding school, which he attended until graduation in 1864. During this time, he and some friends created a literary society called "Germania." Every month, each member submitted and read an essay. They pooled their resources to purchase subscriptions to a popular German musical journal and also bought musical scores. Nietzsche started to suffer eye strains and migraines during this time, problems that would plague him his entire life.

From boarding school, Nietzsche went to the University of Bonn where he intended to concentrate on theology and *philology* (the study and interpretation of classical and Biblical texts). In the 19th century, philology referred to the study of both language and literature. The term is rarely used today because a distinction is drawn between literary and linguistic fields of inquiry.

Influences and College Years

During his days at the University of Bonn, Nietzsche was a student of Wilhelm Ritschl, a distinguished professor of philology and a classics scholar. Ritschl left the university after a feud with another philology professor and went to the University of Leipzig. Nietzsche soon followed him. Ritschl became Nietzsche's mentor and described his intellect:

However many young talents I have seen develop under my eyes for thirty-nine years now, never yet have I know a young man, or tried to help one along in my field as best I could, who was so mature as early and as young as this Nietzsche. . . . If—God grant—that he lives long enough, I prophesy that he will one day stand in the front rank of German philology . . . he possesses the enviable gift of presenting ideas, talking freely, as calmly as he speaks skillfully and clearly. He is the idol, and without wishing it, the leader of the whole younger generation of philologists here in Leipzig . . . and at the same time pleasant and modest (Kaufman, *The Portable Nietzsche*).

Rischl helped Nietzsche publish several articles in the philology journal. Nietzsche also switched his degree from theology to philology; his writings show his movement away from his Lutheran upbringing to an atheistic outlook.

During his college years (1865–1869), Nietzsche encountered many life-altering events, including his reading of Schopenhauer, his contraction of and treatment for syphilis, his year of military service, and his first meeting with Richard Wagner.

Schopenhauer's Will

In 1865, Nietzsche came across a book that changed his life and his philosophy: Schopenhauer's *The World as Will and Representation*. Nietzsche claimed that reading this book turned him into a philosopher, and he founded the Schopenhauer Society in 1911. In this book, Schopenhauer presented his concept of will as the driving force behind life, and Nietzsche expanded and modified this idea into his own "will to power." Schopenhauer was the first openly and explicitly atheistic philosopher, and he was very pessimistic. He thought that life was rife with suffering and said that ". . . so long as we are given up to the throng of desires with its constant hopes and fears . . . we never obtain lasting happiness or peace." He was surprised when he was introduced to Hinduism and Buddhism, because his philosophy shared similar insights to these religions, both arrived at via different paths.

Schopenhauer had a pessimistic outlook on life, and Nietzsche differed here—a difference some critics fail to note. Nietzsche's outlook was life-affirming, and he eventually moved beyond Schopenhauer and his views, although they had a marked influence initially.

A Visit to a Brothel Has Consequences

Also during his university days, Nietzsche is rumored to have visited a brothel, and some surmise that here he contracted syphilis (one of the main attention-grabbing items mentioned about Nietzsche). He was treated for syphilis in 1866, although until the invention of antibiotics, the disease wasn't really that treatable. There is a lot of speculation about when Nietzsche may have contracted this illness, but there is no definitive answer. It is doubtful that he was sexually promiscuous or a homosexual (other myths). It is argued that the doctors who treated him did not tell Nietzsche of the seriousness of the prognosis, because Nietzsche does not mention the disease in any of his writings for the next two decades.

More Bad Luck

In 1867, Nietzsche began his one year of required military service. He first attempted to enlist in a Berlin regiment, but because this regiment was not accepting one-year volunteers like Nietzsche, he instead became part of a mounted field artillery unit near Naumburg. During his military service, he lived at home with his mother.

In the military, he suffered a chest injury when he slammed his chest against the saddle horn after a jump while on horseback. The chest injury did not heal properly until four months later after a visit to a specialist. He returned to Leipzig in the fall of 1868.

This injury added to his syphilis; recurring migraines and eye problems were just the start. Nietzsche suffered additional health problems when he served in the Franco-Prussian War, and his health was always a problem. One of Nietzsche's themes is suffering and its role. Rather than deny his pain, Nietzsche sought to embrace it. He writes in *The Gay Science,* "Whoever commits to paper what he suffers becomes a melancholy author: but he becomes a serious author when he tells us what he suffered and why he now reposes in joy." He also says:

> And as for sickness: would we not almost be tempted to ask whether we can in any way do without it? Only great pain is, as the teacher of great suspicion, the ultimate liberator of the spirit. . . . It is only great pain, that slow protracted pain which takes its time and in which we are as it were burned with green wood, that compels us philosophers to descend into our ultimate depths and to put from us all trust, all that is good-hearted, palliated, gentle, average, wherein perhaps our humanity

previously reposed. I doubt whether such pain "improves"—but I do know it deepens us.

Suffering is a central theme in Nietzsche's work (as you'll read in the next chapter). He suffered not only from bad health, but also from a lack of friends, partners, readers, and money. Suffering is a common theme in philosophy; it is a hallmark of a long list of philosophers who also suffered greatly (sometimes from disease, but often due to persecution for their beliefs).

Friendship with Wagner

One of Nietzsche's more important friendships, one that would affect him for good and bad throughout his life, was his friendship with the composer and musician Richard Wagner (1813–1883). Nietzsche became acquainted with the composer's music during the period of his literary club, Germania. He also knew that Wagner was a fan of the philosophy of Schopenhauer. Nietzsche met the composer in November 1868.

Wagner played an important role in Nietzsche's life. He was about the same age as Nietzsche's father would have been; they were both born in the same year. He also had attended the University of Leipzig. Nietzsche visited and spent a lot of time with Wagner and his wife, Cosima, at their Swiss home in Tirbschen, a small town near Lucerne, and in Bayreuth, Germany.

Initially, Nietzsche thought that Wagner represented the ideals he espoused in *The Birth of Tragedy,* a work that Wagner greatly praised. Later, he became disillusioned with Wagner's misuse of religious sentimentality and his hypocrisy, especially in Wagner's *Parsifal.* He also disagreed with Wagner's anti-Semitism. He broke painfully with his mentor and, in his last days, wrote two works addressing their relationship. Nietzsche lost other friendships during his life and suffered, in addition to his physical ailments, a deep loneliness. A reader can find many places where Nietzsche addresses his loneliness, as in this quotation from *Twilight of the Idols:* "To live alone, one must be either an animal or a god—says Aristotle. Leaving out the third possibility: one must be both—a philosopher."

Professor Nietzsche

Right around the time that Nietzsche met Wagner, Ritschl recommended Nietzsche for a position at the University of Basel, and in 1869, the

University of Basel took that recommendation, making Nietzsche a professor of classical philosophy. In an unusual gesture, the University of Leipzig awarded Nietzsche a Ph.D. without a dissertation. Nietzsche began his teaching career at the age of 24.

He continued to teach there for ten years although the academic life did not suit him. He taught classes such as Greek Lyric Poets, Latin Grammar, Introduction to the Study of Plato, and Sophocles's *Oedipus Rex*. He took a leave to serve as a volunteer in the Franco-Prussian War, and he began his publishing career.

A Medical Orderly in the Franco-Prussian War

Nietzsche served as a volunteer medical orderly in 1870 after the outbreak of the Franco-Prussian War. His ill health again affected his service; he contracted dysentery and diphtheria and returned to teaching. These additional illnesses added to his already problematic health, and his health never recovered.

His First Books

During his tenure at the University of Basel, Nietzsche published several essays, but his first major work, *The Birth of Tragedy from the Spirit of Music*, was published in 1872. This book argues that the Apollonian elements of reason, logic, and order have overtaken the Western world to the world's detriment. A better alternative is a balance of these elements and Dionysian elements, including instinctual, wild, creative forces. Nietzsche thought that these forces were best represented in contemporary German music. (You can read more about this work in Chapter 3.) Wagner praised the book, but it did not receive the same welcome from scholars.

His friendship with Wagner was beginning to show strains with Nietzsche's second book, *Human, All-Too-Human* (1878), which he completed during the end of his university career. The characterization of "the artist" is said to represent Wagner.

The Wander Years

Nietzsche did not enjoy the life of the academic; he often criticizes this lifestyle. In *Thus Spoke Zarathustra,* he writes "I am not, like them, trained to pursue knowledge as if it were nutcracking." He criticizes them descriptively in this passage from *Thus Spoke Zarathustra:*

> They are good clockworks; but take care to wind them correctly! Then they indicate the hour without fail and make a modest noise. They work like mills and stamps: throw down your seed-corn to them and they will know how to grind it small and reduce it to white dust.

He resigned his university position in 1879, because of poor health. His first book alienated Nietzsche from his mentor, Ritschl, the academic community, and his students, and it was probably this as much as his illness, which led him to retire. From that point on, he devoted his life to writing. From 1879 to January 1889, he traveled and spent time in various locations, from boarding houses in Switzerland to the French Riviera, and all over Italy (Turin, Genoa, Florence, Venice, Rome, Rapallo). He published *Daybreak* (1881), *The Gay Science* (1882), *Thus Spoke Zarathustra* (1883 and 1885), *Beyond Good and Evil* (1886), and *On the Genealogy of Morals* (1887). Many of these works were published using his own money, and none had a big audience. He also finished in his last active year *Ecce Homo, Twilight of the Idols, The Case of Wagner, The Anti-Christ,* and *Nietzsche Contra Wagner,* a great volume of work produced in only a few years by an ill man who was essentially an invalid.

Unrequited Love

Nietzsche was devoted to writing, and he did not have a very active love life. He had only one substantial love interest. At age 37, he met and fell in love with Lou Salomé, a 21-year-old Russian student. She was in Zurich studying philosophy and theology. Nietzsche proposed marriage, but Salomé declined. She was more interested in Nietzsche's friend, Paul Rée, a psychologist. Later Salomé would become the mistress of poet Rainer Maria Rilke and the confidant of Sigmund Freud. She would also write of her relationship with Nietzsche.

In 1876, Nietzsche had earlier proposed marriage to Mathilde Trampedach, a Dutch piano student in Geneva, but she had also declined.

Descent into Madness

In January 1889, Nietzsche had a mental breakdown when he witnessed a coachman beating an old horse in the street in Turin, Italy. A friend brought him from Italy back to Basel, and he spent the last years of his life in an asylum in Basel, under his mother's care. When his mother died in 1897, his sister took over his care (moving him to a different location) until his death on August 25, 1900. He died of pneumonia and is buried in Roecken, the town where he was born. Nietzsche died before he had the opportunity to fully develop his thinking.

The Nazi Sister

Nietzsche's sister, Elisabeth, took and maintained control over his estate and used it for her own personal agenda. Elisabeth was married to Bernhard Forster, and they had moved to Paraguay to start an Aryan, anti-Semitic German colony called "New Germany." They were leading anti-Semites, a view Nietzsche did *not* share. The colony failed, and Forster committed suicide. Elisabeth returned home to Germany, yet this did not stop Elisabeth from using Nietzsche's writing for her own purpose.

Elisabeth published several of his works after his collapse, including *The Anti-Christ* and *Nietzsche Contra Wagner.* These works are not as much in doubt as is *The Will to Power,* which was published from collected notes and published in 1901. It was also Elisabeth who aligned herself with Hitler and invited him to the Nietzsche Archive. Nietzsche did not support Nazism; his writing shows he opposed any such ideas. He lived most of his life outside of Germany and was not an anti-Semite. He did make comments and was interested in the origins of Christianity from Judaism, both positive and negative. In *Human, All-Too-Human,* he praise the Jewish race:

> [I]n the darkest time of the Middle Ages, when the Asiatic cloud masses had gathered heavily over Europe, it was Jewish free-thinkers, scholars, and physicians who clung to the banner of enlightenment and spiritual independence in the face of the harshest personal pressures and defended Europe against Asia. We owe it to their exertions . . . that the bond of culture which now links us with the enlightenment of Greco-Roman antiquity remains unbroken.

He also did not advocate a German Aryan master race (related to his version of superman) or the annihilation of Jews.

In the end, Nietzsche died alone, misunderstood, unacclaimed, and unaware of the immense impact he would have on future generations of thinkers, scholars, writers, and philosophers. He came nowhere close to the ideal death he imagined and described in *Twilight of the Idols:*

To die proudly when it is no longer possible to live proudly. Death freely chosen, death at the right time, brightly and cheerfully accomplished amid children and witnesses: then a real farewell is still possible, as the one who is taking leave is still there; also a real estimate of what one has wished, drawing the sum of one's life—all in opposition to the wretched and revolting comedy that Christianity has made of the hour of death.

Yet, he did achieve something else he strived for, cited in the same book *(Twilight of the Idols):* "To create things on which time tests its teeth in vain; in form, in substance, to strive for a little immorality—I have never yet been modest enough to demand less of myself."

2 Nietzsche's Philosophy

I would believe only in a god who could dance.

—Nietzsche, *Thus Spoke Zarathustra*

Because a lot of controversy surrounds Nietzsche, a reader can begin with a lot of misconceptions about his work. When exploring his writing, though, the reader might be surprised to find it funny, challenging, and relevant today. His work is immensely readable (although demanding). This chapter gives an overview of Nietzsche's works and key themes.

Nietzsche's Works

During the sixteen years from the publication of his first book to when he went insane, Nietzsche wrote several books, and his writing may not be what readers expect from a philosopher. It is funny, vivid, personal, poetic, challenging, at times seemingly contradictory, deceptively simple, and still very relevant to the world today. His aphoristic works are easy to read, but don't be deceived: If you think about them, you at once recognize the depth and relevance of the thought. This section discusses some influences on Nietzsche and his writing style, as well as lists his works with a short description.

Influenced By . . .

Nietzsche said that he decided to become a philosopher after reading the German philosopher Schopenhauer (1788–1860), and Nietzsche agreed with much of Schopenhauer's philosophical ideas. Schopenhauer was known as the "philosopher of pessimism" because he believed the empirical world was without reason or purpose. In his work, *The World as Will and Representation,* Schopenhauer continued and clarified concepts of reality forwarded by Kant, provided an argument that it was through art (especially music) that one could find relief from the suffering of life, and said the entire world consisted of an expanding, unknowable, purposeless energy or force that he called *will.*

Nietzsche's friendship with the composer Wagner was based on a shared admiration of the philosophy of Schopenhauer. Nietzsche particularly picked up on the ideas of will and the lack of an all-powerful and all-knowing God. He also thought art, in particular music, played a vital role in finding meaning in life. As he developed his philosophy, though, he significantly deviated from Schopenhauer. Mainly, Nietzsche offered an affirmative view of life, rather than a pessimistic one.

In addition to Schopenhauer, Nietzsche was also influenced by Darwin and his theory of evolution—again, with some differences. Nietzsche thought that it was not the struggle for existence that drove evolution, but the struggle for greatness. You can see his theory of evolution in his idea of superman as well as the genealogy of morals (covered later in this chapter).

Nietzsche also greatly admired the Greek philosopher Heraclitus, famous for saying, "You can't step into the same river twice." He agreed with his ideas of the continuity of life and liked his concept that the whole universe is like fire and consists of flashes. Nietzsche modified this idea, substituting *force* or *will* for *fire.*

His Writing Style

In Nietzsche's early career, he wrote mostly essays, and his writing was clear, vivid, and intelligent. In mid-career, he started writing *aphorisms,* short pieces—sometimes one paragraph, sometimes several—that express a general truth. He also wrote a fictional account of the wandering sage Zarathustra. At the end of his career, he returned again to essays.

All of Nietzsche's work showed his knowledge of contemporary, classic, and Biblical texts. He stressed the importance of good writing, and he was an excellent writer himself. Of aphorisms, he writes

A good aphorism is too hard for the teeth of time and is not eaten up by all the centuries, even though it serves as food for every age: hence it is the greatest paradox in literature, the imperishable in the midst of change, the nourishment which—like salt—is always prized, but which never loses its savor as salt does *(Mixed Opinions and Maxims).*

And of writing in general, he says, "[I]t is my ambition to say in ten sentences what everyone else says in a book—what everyone else does not say in a book" *(Twilight of the Idols)*.

As a writer, Nietzsche is very funny, and he particularly stressed the importance of humor. He loved plays on words (which are sometimes lost in the translation), and his writing is colorful and poetic. He makes his points using vibrant imagery: "You stand there honorable and stiff and with straight backs, you famous wise men: no strong wind will drive you. Have you never seen a sail go over the sea, rounded and taut and trembling with the violence of the wind?" *(Thus Spoke Zarathustra)*. Or in another passage: "Our treasure lies in the beehive of our knowledge. We are perpetually on the way thither, being by nature winged insects and honey gatherers of the mind" *(The Genealogy of Morals)*.

A modern reader will find that his words of advice are still pertinent today. For instance, he writes, "When marrying, one should ask oneself this question: Do you believe that you will be able to converse well with this woman into your old age? Everything else in a marriage is transitory" *(Human, All-Too-Human)*.

Nietzsche also showed his keen psychological insights in his writing. As an example, consider this tidbit from *Thus Spoke Zarathustra:* "Our faith in other betrays in what respect we would like to have faith in ourselves" *(Thus Spoke Zarathustra)*.

Nietzsche's Key Works

Nietzsche published his first work at the age of 28, and he wrote continuously up to 1888, when he went mad at the age of 44. The following are his major works:

- *The Birth of Tragedy* (1872) was Nietzsche's first book. This essay-style work traces the beginnings of tragedy, the triumph of rationalism (associated with Apollo, the Greek god of order and reason) over aesthetic experience (influences of Dionysus, the Greek god of wine), and why passion needs to be reintroduced into modern culture. You can read more about this work in Chapter 3.

- *Untimely Meditations* (1873–1875) is a series of essays published on history, David Strauss (a theologian), Richard Wagner, and Schopenhauer.

- *Human, All-Too-Human* (1878) was written after Nietzsche broke his relationship with Wagner and also began to separate his thinking from the views of Schopenhauer, gaining his own voice in this work. He later published two sequels, *Mixed Opinions and Maxims* (1879) and *The Wanderer and His Shadow* (1880); both were also collections of aphorisms. The original and the sequels were published together in 1886 with the title *Human, All-Too-Human, A Book for Free Spirits.*

- *Daybreak* or *The Dawn* (1881) stayed with the aphoristic style and discussed the importance of the feeling of power. In this work, you can see the beginnings of Nietzsche's concept of the will to power. *The Stanford Encyclopedia of Philosophy* calls this work "his intellectually calmest, and most intimate."

- *The Gay Science* (1882) was another collection of aphorisms. It is the work in which Nietzsche proclaimed "God is dead," and is the first place Nietzsche discusses the concept of "eternal recurrence" and many other of his well-known ideas.

- *Thus Spoke Zarathustra* (1883–1885) marks a change in Nietzsche's writing style. This work tells the story of the wise and lonely wanderer (much like Nietzsche himself) as he relates parables, advice, and collected wisdom. This is the most famous and popular of Nietzsche's works. Consisting of four parts, the works were published over several years. Parts I and II were published in 1883, Part III in 1884, Part IV in 1885. More were planned but never completed. Chapter 5 highlights this important work.

- *Beyond Good and Evil* (1886) reevaluates the concept of values as "good" or "bad." He takes a viewpoint "beyond good and evil"— that is, from "the perspective of life"—and writes "a natural history of morals." In Chapter 6, you can find a summary of this work.

- *Genealogy of Morals* (1887) consists of three essays and has three basic purposes: continue to describe the history of morals, analyze the origin of "bad conscience" and guilt, and critique these morals. In this work, Nietzsche relates his ideas of slave and master moralities.

- *The Case of Wagner* (1888) shows off Nietzsche's talents as a music critic, as he disparages his once friend and mentor, Richard Wagner.

- *Twilight of the Idols* (1888, 1889), with the subtitle *How One Philosophizes with a Hammer,* includes Nietzsche's critique of many "idols" including the philosophers Socrates, Plato, and Kant, as well as other famous British, Italian, and French noted individuals. Those singled out as worthy of praise include Caesar, Napoleon, Goethe, and Dostoevski. This work as well as the next three in this list were written before Nietzsche went insane but published later.

- *Nietzsche Contra Wagner* (1888, 1889), completed just weeks before his mental breakdown, contrasts his views with Wagner's, emphasizing how someone can become corrupted, especially by Christianity.

- *The Anti-Christ* (1888, 1894) was intended as the first of four parts of the unfinished *Revaluation of All Values.* In this short work, Nietzsche openly attacks Christian culture and its influence on values. Nietzsche portrays Jesus in a positive light; according to Nietzsche, it is Paul who is the villain of Christianity.

- *Ecce Homo* (1888, 1908) is an autobiographical work with such interesting headings as "Why I Am So Wise" and "Why I Am So Clever." In this sarcastic review of life and works, Nietzsche includes portions of his earlier works and provides insight on the inspiration for his work as well as a critique of his work. This work is the focus of Chapter 7.

- *The Will to Power* (1888, 1901), published by his sister, is a collection of his notes, some already used, some significantly edited by his sister. Like the other works his sister published, critics have questioned the validity of this work.

The Controversy of Later Works

In addition to *The Will to Power,* Nietzsche's sister published various fragments, letters, and essays after his death. There is much debate about how this work should be interpreted, because it isn't clear whether Nietzsche intended them for publication. Some believe he kept private his more personal views, giving more weight to these works. Others disagree, saying these ideas were not as polished or fully developed; therefore, the published works are emphasized and the others read with a somewhat skeptical eye. Yet others treat all the work equally. As a reader, you may want to take this into consideration when reading any of these works and form your own opinion; it's most likely what Nietzsche would have recommended.

Nietzsche's Themes

Nietzsche is not a systematic philosopher; that is, he does not develop one system of philosophy that encompasses all his ideas. In fact, he writes "I mistrust all systematizers and avoid them. The will to a system is a lack of integrity" *(Twilight of the Idols)*. His philosophy is relevant to life, not abstract ideas, and he challenges, critiques, analyzes, and describes many, many aspects of life. This section discusses Nietzsche's key themes.

His works are unique because each one does not address one or two themes; instead, they are interrelated. Themes and ideas from previous works are echoed throughout all following work. Walter Kaufmann, one of the best-known editors and translators of Nietzsche, writes that ". . . each book is part of the man, and the resulting existential unity makes all of them part of a single work" *(The Portable Nietzsche)*.

The Quest for Truth

Rather than abstract, irrelevant issues, Nietzsche said we should be concerned with everyday life. He writes in his criticism of the existing historical works, "Where is there a history of love, avarice, envy, conscience, piety, cruelty?" *(The Gay Science)*. He offers a different way to approach and evaluate knowledge.

To start, he voices his concerns about the limits of science as the be-all and end-all of truth and warns against science becoming the new religion. He points out that although scientists can better describe things, they really can't explain them any better. For instance, in *The Gay Science* he writes

> Assuming that one estimated the value of a piece of music according to how much of it could be counted, calculated, and expressed in formulas: how absurd would such a "scientific" estimation of music be! What would one have comprehended, understood, grasped of it? Nothing, really nothing of what is "music."

He asks, "Do we really want to permit existence to be degraded like this—reduced to a mere exercise for a calculator and an indoor diversion for mathematics?" This knowledge is "human, all-too-human," and Nietzsche says "an essentially mechanical world would be an essentially meaningless world" *(The Gay Science)*. He also shows that for any given event there are many interpretations. He challenges the idea of causality and the so called "laws" of nature.

He also questions and asks his readers to question what purpose the knowledge serves. Is it relevant? Of all knowledge, he stressed self-knowledge, which is the most difficult. (His concepts can be interpreted to equate all knowledge with self-knowledge.) He thought that self-knowledge would enable one to live happily and freely. Other types of knowledge can be employed for this reason: "Let us introduce the refinement and rigor of mathematics into all science as far as this is possible, not in the faith that this will lead us to know things, but in order to *determine* our human relation to things" *(The Gay Science).*

God Is Dead

In *The Gay Science,* Nietzsche relates the story of the madman who lit a lantern and went to the marketplace seeking God and then says, "'I seek God! I seek God! . . . God is dead. God remains dead. And we have killed him.'" The madman concludes that he has come too soon and says "'What are these churches now if they are not the tombs and sepulchers of God?'"

Nietzsche simply does not believe in an eternal, all-knowing, omnipotent, judging, morally right God. He does not believe in a world beyond this one, and he seeks to show his readers the way the concept of "God" has been used. In *Daybreak,* he writes that God has been used "to darken the heavens, to blot out the sun, to cast suspicion on joy, to deprive hope of its value, to paralyze the active hand."

He gives an acerbic description of this god:

A god who begets children with a mortal woman; a sage who bids men work no more, have no more courts, but look for signs of the impending end of the world; a justice that accepts the innocent as a vicarious sacrifice; someone who orders his disciples to drink his blood; prayers for miraculous intervention; sins perpetrated against a god, atoned for by a god, fear of a beyond which death is the portal; the form of the cross as a symbol in time that no longer knows the function and the ignominy of the cross *(Human, All-Too-Human).*

He especially dislikes the emphasis on suffering as punishment and the vengefulness of Christianity. In *Daybreak,* he writes, "Only in Christendom did everything become punishment, well-deserved punishment: it also makes the sufferer's imagination suffer, so that with every misfortune, he feels himself morally reprehensible and cast out."

Despite his attack on Christianity, he did admire Jesus and writes, "Would that he had remained in the wilderness and far from the good and the just! Perhaps he would have learned to live and to love the earth—and laughter, too!" *(Thus Spoke Zarathustra)*. In the anti-Christ, he cites Jesus's words, "The kingdom of God is in you," to say that eternal life is here on earth, not in some other nonexistent world.

Nietzsche describes how one should live, here on Earth.

Live Here, on Earth

Nietzsche stresses this life here on Earth. He takes issue with the portrayal of earthly life as evil and ugly and the reliance on and anticipation of some other life or other world beyond this one. He says that "it was suffering and incapacity that created all afterworlds" and advises his reader in *Thus Spoke Zarathustra* to "no longer bury one's head in the sand of heavenly things, but to bear it freely, an earthly head, which creates a meaning for the earth." He writes further that "man has felt too little joy; that alone, my brothers, is our original sin. And learning better to feel joy, we learn best not to hurt others or to plan hurts for them" *(Thus Spoke Zarathustra)*.

He is angered by the self-hatred and resulting feelings of resentment and guilt and seeks to transform that to an affirmation of life. He urges his readers to embrace the things they have been led to believe are bad or evil (their bodies, their sexuality, for instance). He writes ". . . the secret of the greatest fruitfulness and the greatest enjoyment of existence is: to live dangerously! Build your cities under Vesuvius! Send your ships into uncharted seas!" *(The Gay Science)*. He associates this life with the Dionysian aspects and often uses the term *amor fati* ("love of fate").

A Life Well Lived

He describes *amor fati* in this passage from *The Gay Science:*

> My formula for greatness in a human being is *amor fati:* that one wants nothing to be other than it is, not in the future, not in the past, not in eternity. Not merely to endure that which happens out of necessity, still less to pretend it isn't real—but to love it.

His view of life without a god is not negative, pessimistic, or nihilistic. He finds it joyful and full of possibility:

Indeed, we philosophers and "free spirits" feel, when we hear the news that the "old god is dead," as if a new dawn shone on us; our heart overflows with gratitude, amazement, premonitions, expectation. At long last the horizon appears free to us again, even if it should not be bright; at long last our ships may venture out again, venture out to face any danger; all the daring of the lover of knowledge is permitted again; the sea, *our* sea, lies open again; perhaps there has never yet been such an "open sea" *(The Gay Science).*

He challenges readers to know themselves and "to become who you are," as well as to strive to become better, more noble. He challenges his writers to make their lives a work of art. And in doing so, be sure to give style to one's character, as described here:

"Giving style" to one's character . . . is exercised by those who see all the strengths and weaknesses of their own natures and then comprehend them in an artistic plan. . . . Here the ugly which could not have been removed is hidden; there it has been reinterpreted and made sublime. . . . For one thing is needful: that a human being attain his satisfaction with himself" *(The Gay Science).*

Life Again and Again

Life on earth can be fulfilling and full of promises, and it had better be because, Nietzsche says with his idea of eternal recurrence, first introduced in *The Gay Science,* one lives the same life over and over. He tells the story of a demon who says to you after sneaking into your "loneliest loneliness":

"This life as you now live it and have lived it, you will have to live once more and innumerable times more; and there will be nothing new in it, but every pain and every joy and every thought and sigh and everything immeasurably small or great in your life must return to you—all in the same succession and sequence." . . . Would you not throw yourself down and gnash your teeth and curse the demon who spoke thus? Or did you once experience a tremendous moment when you would have answered him, "You are a god, and never have I heard anything more godly." If this thought were to gain possession of you, it would change you, as you are, or perhaps crush you" *(The Gay Science).*

Faced with this life view, it's all the more important to make the most of this life.

The Will to Power

For Nietzsche, man's main drive is not the will to exist, and he relates how this logically does not make sense: "For, what does not exist cannot will; but what is in existence, how could that still want existence? Only where there is life is there also will: not will to live but . . . will to power" *(Thus Spoke Zarathustra).* In many of his works, he discusses this will: "[I]n me there is something invulnerable and unburiable, something that explodes rock: that is *my will"* *(Thus Spoke Zarathustra).* He connects the goal of life to will: "What is genius?—To will both a lofty goal and the means to achieving it" *(Human, All-Too-Human).*

Superman!

The goal, Nietzsche says, is to strive to become a better, more noble person, and in his works he describes this potential evolution of man. To Nietzsche, man was currently "a rope tied between beast and superman—a rope over an abyss." Nietzsche says that "man is something that shall be overcome" *(Thus Spoke Zarathustra).* He challenges, "Could you *create* a god? Then do not speak to me of any gods. But you could well create the superman" *(Thus Spoke Zarathustra).* This superman (*Ubermensch* in German and also translated as "overman") is not a given, but a challenge, a goal, an ideal. He writes, "Let your will say: The superman shall be the meaning of the earth."

Good versus Bad

If the world has no value (that is, value is in heaven), how can life have value? Nietzsche believes this life *does* have value; he does not believe in some other world in which one gets his or her reward for a life well lived. And if there is no God, there can be no ultimate moral or value system. Without God to tell us what is good and what is bad, we must decide for ourselves. So Nietzsche questions all virtues and values and encourages his readers to do the same.

He turns the idea of common virtues on their heads, pointing out that most virtues are praised because they are helpful to someone else but actually harmful to yourself. He says, "Instead of expending their strength and reason on their own preservation, evolution, or advancement—they expend it on ours." You'll find Nietzsche describing how existing values are created, challenging their accepted meaning, and offering alternative moral theories in many of his works.

The Herd versus the Individual

Throughout his writing, Nietzsche stresses the individual—the individual over the herd, the individual striving to be something more, the individual seeking knowledge of him- or herself, the individual creating his or her own morals. The importance of the individual is the main tenet of Existentialism. (Søren Kierkegaard, a Danish philosopher, is cited as the "Father of Existentialism." For more information on this key philosopher, consider *Kierkegaard Within Your Grasp,* also published by Wiley.) Nietzsche writes, "All our actions are altogether incomparably personal, unique, and infinitely individual" *(The Gay Science).*

Nietzsche also uses the concept of the herd and the individual to discuss man's evolution as well as his morals. In his theory, the individual is the aberration, and Nietzsche fears the individuals will be stamped out by the herd and become obsolete. He explains the way morals are created and the positive impact of an individual:

> History teaches that the best-preserved tribe among a people is the one in which most men have a living communal sense as a consequence of sharing their customary and indisputable principles . . . here the subordination of the individual is learned. . . . The danger to these strong communities founded on homogeneous individuals who have character is growing stupidity, which is gradually increased by heredity . . . they loosen up and from time to time inflict a wound on the stable element of a community. Precisely in this wounded and weakened spot the whole structure is *inoculated* as it were, with something new *(Human, All-Too-Human).*

The herd conforms, coordinates, and collaborates to create a value system that they all then uphold. He writes, "[M]an's greatest labor so far has been to reach agreement about very many things and to submit it to a law of agreement—regardless of whether these things are true or false" *(The Gay Science).* Morality doesn't come from God; it comes from social convention and customs.

Master and Slave

In his quest to trace morality, Nietzsche also discusses how virtues have evolved (the genealogy of morals), and he presents two types of individuals—master and slave—with two different ethical codes. (These terms, unfortunately, have a negative connotation, but Nietzsche did not mean them that way.

Also note that, without understanding the whole of his master-and-slave-relationship system, it is easy to pull out bits and pieces and to create a much different picture than Nietzsche intended.)

The master commands and obeys only his own will. He is "good." The slave obeys the master, and he is "bad" (in this case, *bad* does not mean evil but weak, cowardly, indecisive). The masters are leaders and strive to excel. The slaves follow out of fear and resentment. In their morals, the master is "bad" and they are "good."

Nietzsche uses Christianity as the worst example of slave morality, and he describes how the virtues or values of the master—for example boldness—are flipped by religion to stress the opposite—for instance, meekness.

Nietzsche's Impact Far and Wide

Nietzsche was brilliantly gifted, yet this brilliance was not publicly recognized during his lifetime. None of his works were enthusiastically received, and it wasn't until George Brandes, the same Danish critic who read and promoted Kierkegaard's ideas, lectured on Nietzsche that he was "discovered." Since that time, he has influenced many individuals, the course of philosophy, and other fields of study.

Nietzsche influenced thinkers and scholars as well as artists of all types. To name a few, Nietzsche impacted writers such as Franz Kafka, author of *Metamorphosis;* Albert Camus, author of *The Outsider;* playwrights George Bernard Shaw and August Strindberg; and poet Rainer Maria Rilke. His influence affected the work of other philosophers including Martin Heidegger, Jean-Paul Sartre, Jacques Derrida, and Michel Foucault. His ideas influenced the development of Existentialism, Deconstruction, and Postmodernism.

Nietzsche also affected many other fields of study, including linguistics, sociology, history, and others. His writings on ego, resentment, conscience, and other psychoanalytical topics affected Freud. His influence and writing are still very valid today, and he remains exciting to read.

Reading Nietzsche

Because much of Nietzsche's work is presented in manageable sections (some as short as a paragraph), it is easy to think that the idea is simple, yet it is most often the opposite—deep and complex. Also, Nietzsche does not focus on a single theme (or two) within a work; instead, he continues his philosophy across all his works. A reader needs to keep the interdependence of his works in mind. Finally, Nietzsche may state something but mean it sarcastically.

In *What Nietzsche Really Said,* Robert Solomon and Kathleen Higgens provide some great advice on reading Nietzsche. They tell the reader to ask him or herself to consider the following:

- Is the concept consistent with other things Nietzsche has written about the same topic? If it's not, has he changed his mind? Or is he offering the contradiction to provide some insight?

- Is Nietzsche praising someone? Attacking someone? If so, what is he trying to say beyond this? Also, Nietzsche often mimics the writing style of others and references classic and Biblical passages. Is he doing so in praise? Or criticism?

- What do the imagery, the metaphors, the symbols offer additionally to the idea?

- Is Nietzsche serious? Or is he poking fun? Is he sarcastic? Exaggerating? If so, to what effect?

With this overview and these guidelines, you're now prepared to consider some of Nietzsche's key works, covered in the chapters that follow.

3 The Birth of Tragedy

*Man . . . always remains attached to the
past: however far and fast he runs, the
chain runs with him.*
—Nietzsche, *On the Uses and Disadvantages
of History for Life*

The Birth of Tragedy: Out of the Spirit of Music was Nietzsche's first work,
published in 1872, while Nietzsche was a professor at the University of
Basel. This work is recognized now as one of the most influential studies
of tragedy, but it was not as critically acclaimed when he published it. Nietzsche's writing style did not follow the typical orthodox academic style; he
argued, poeticized, included anecdotes, and used metaphors in this work.

Although the work may not appeal to modern readers unless they're
familiar with Greek writers such as Archilochus, Euripides, Homer, Aeschy-
lus, and others, it does show the beginnings of Nietzsche's philosophy. Also,
because Nietzsche is commenting on ancient work—work that is the basis
of Western civilization—it is also of interest to modern readers. Finally, the
"Attempt at a Self-Criticism" that Nietzsche added to *The Birth of Tragedy*
in 1886, fourteen years after its original publication, is enlightening. This
chapter describes this, the first of Nietzsche's works.

What Nietzsche Argues in The Birth of Tragedy

In *The Birth of Tragedy*, Nietzsche seeks to find the relation of art to science.
In doing so, he looks at the two distinct and important figures from Greek
mythology: Apollo and Dionysus. He uses these Greek gods and what they
represent to show how both forces are necessary and fundamental.

Nietzsche says that Apollo, the god of order and reason, finds his best expression in temples and sculpture. Apollo represents restraint, measure, harmony, and optimism.

In contrast to Apollo, Dionysus, the god of wine and partying, is associated with sensual abandon, music, and intoxication. In the ecstatic dance that Dionysus calls one to, that person finds release from isolation.

Nietzsche argues that these two forces reached a synthesis in tragedy, and it is realized "what potentially destructive forces had to be harnessed to make them [tragedies] possible." From this, Nietzsche argues that a life philosophy requires elements from both reason and the tragic aspect of life.

The Birth of Tragedy includes twenty-five sections. The first six set the stage and introduce the main assumptions for the argument. Parts 7 through 15 are the critical parts of the book. The remaining sections were tacked on, and Nietzsche himself regrets the addition (discussed later). This section discusses what Nietzsche argues in this work.

Setting the Stage

In his self-critique of the work, Nietzsche posed some of the questions he sought to answer in this work:

- "Is pessimism *necessarily* a sign of decline, decay, degeneration, weary and weak instincts?"

- "Is there a pessimism of *strength*?"

- "And science itself, our science—indeed, what is the significance of all science viewed as a symptom of life?"

He strives to look at "the problem of science itself, presented in the context of art" or, as he also says, "*to look at science in the perspective of the artist, but at art in that of life*" (*The Birth of Tragedy*).

To argue this point, he discusses the development of tragedy and the inclusion and change of emphasis from Apollonian and Dionysian influences. It's Nietzsche's contention that the "continuous development of art is bound up with the *Apollinian* and *Dionysian* duality." He says that these two influences "continually incite each other to new and more powerful births." And the ultimate achievement of the intermingling of the two life views "create an equally Dionysian and Apollinian form of art—Attic tragedy."

Nietzsche starts by discussing Apollo and his association with the dream world. He says that "in the creation of" dream worlds, "every man is truly an artist." He describes Apollo as the shining one, "the deity of light" and calls him the "ruler over the beautiful illusion of the inner world of fantasy." He also emphasizes the individual, citing Apollo as "the glorious divine image of the *principium individuationis* [principle of individuation]."

He contrasts this principle of the individual to Dionysus in which "each one feels himself not only united, reconciled, and fused with his neighbor, but as one with him." He says that "in song and dance man expresses himself as a member of a higher community." He particularly stresses the impact of music: "Dionysian *music* in particular excited awe and terror."

He sums up these connections and the movement from the individual (Apollo and his dream world) to connection with others and ultimately oneself:

> As artistic energies which burst forth from nature herself, *without the mediation of the human artist*—energies in which nature's art impulses are satisfied in the most immediate and direct way—first in the image world of dreams, whose completeness is not dependent upon the intellectual attitude or the artistic culture of any single being; and then as intoxicated reality, which likewise, does not heed the single unit, but even seeks to destroy the individual and redeem him by a mystic feeling of oneness *(The Birth of Tragedy)*.

He shows how knowledge of pain and suffering is transformed. He starts by relating the story of Midas who captured Silenus, the companion of Dionysus, and asked what is the best and most desirable thing for man. Silenus answered him, "What is best of all is utterly beyond your reach: not to be born, not to *be,* to be *nothing.* But the second best for you is—to die soon." Nietzsche says, "The Greeks knew and felt the terror and horror of existence."

Nietzsche says, though, that art is created by necessity from this knowledge:

> All this again and again overcome by the Greeks with the aid of the Olympian *middle world* of art; or at any rate it was veiled and withdrawn from sight. It was in order to be able to live that the Greeks had to create these gods from a most profound need.

He also argues that art can have a transformative power. He writes that the Greeks "triumphed over an abysmal and terrifying view of the world and keenest susceptibility to suffering through recourse to the most forceful and pleasurable illusions." In doing so, the Greeks, rather than wishing for death, transformed that desire into one for life:

> Existence under the bright sunshine of such gods is regarded as desirable in itself, and the real pain of Homeric men is caused by parting from it, especially by early parting: so that now, reversing the wisdom of Silenus, we might say of the Greeks that "to die soon is worst of all for them, the next worst—to die at all."

From Suffering to Art

The first sections of *The Birth of Tragedy* describe the influences that went into the origin of Greek tragedy. Nietzsche then goes on to trace the development of tragedy and offers the prevailing view *"that tragedy arose from the tragic chorus."* He discusses the role of the chorus, discounting other ideas that the chorus is the "ideal spectator" and that the chorus "represents the people in contrast to the aristocratic region of the scene."

He calls the "chorus in its primitive form, in proto-tragedy, the mirror image in which the Dionysian man contemplates himself." Nietzsche says that this mirror enables one "to see oneself transformed before one's own eyes and to begin to act as if one had actually entered into another body, another character. This process stands at the beginning of the origins of drama." He continues this argument stating that, "We realize that the scene, complete with the action, was basically and originally thought of merely as a *vision;* the chorus is the only 'reality' and generates the vision."

Nietzsche next says that "In its vision this chorus beholds its lord and master Dionysus and is therefore eternally the *serving* chorus: it sees how the god suffers and glorifies himself and therefore does not itself *act.*" And he sums up, an argument that will form the basis of his philosophy, that *"sharing his suffering* it also shares something of his *wisdom* and proclaims the truth from the heart of the world." Nietzsche finds the power and potential in suffering.

He emphasizes the importance of art, and his theory of art is one of his cited philosophical tenets. He writes

> With this chorus the profound Hellene, uniquely susceptible to the tenderest and deepest suffering, comforts himself, having looked boldly right into the terrible destructiveness of so-called world history as well

as the cruelty of nature, and being in danger of long for a Buddhistic negation of the will. Art saves him, and through art—life.

He provides a brilliant explanation of this theory of suffering and knowledge, using Hamlet as his example:

> In this sense the Dionysian man resembles Hamlet: both have once looked truly into the essence of things, they have gained *knowledge,* and nausea inhibits action; for their action could not change anything in the eternal nature of things; they feel it to be ridiculous and humiliating that they should be asked to set right a world that is out of joint. Knowledge kills action; action requires the veils of illusion: that is the doctrine of Hamlet, not that cheap wisdom of Jack the Dreamer who reflects too much and, as it were, from an excess of possibilities does not get around to action. Not reflection, no—true knowledge, an insight into the horrible truth outweighs any motive for action, both in Hamlet and in the Dionysian man.

He sums up his arguments:

> This view of things already provides us with all the elements of a profound and pessimistic view of the world, together with the *mystery doctrine of tragedy;* the fundamental knowledge of oneness of everything existent, the conception of individuation as the primal cause of evil, and of art as the joyous hope that the spell of individuation may be broken in augury of a restored oneness.

And again he stresses the role of art: "when the danger to his will is greatest, *art* approaches as a saving sorceress, expert at healing."

Socrates and the Death of Tragedy

From the birth of tragedy, Nietzsche goes on to discuss its death, saying Greek tragedy "died by suicide." He points the finger at the Greek playwright Euripides because he "brought the *spectator* onto the stage" and "through him the everyday man forced his way from the spectators' seats onto the stage." Doing so meant that "everyday life could be represented on the stage" and that Euripides "thus qualified him [the spectator] to pass judgment on the drama."

How did Euripides come to this new approach? Nietzsche surmises that he sat in the theater and watched other dramas, dramas by his acclaimed predecessors. But what he found in these works is that he didn't always understand the outcome. Solutions to ethical problems were not clear-cut, good and bad fortunes were not parsed out fairly. Therefore, he decided "to reconstruct tragedy purely on the basis of an un-Dionysian art, morality, and world view."

Nietzsche also cites the influence of the "demon Socrates." He describes "aesthetic Socratism, whose supreme law reads roughly as follows, 'To be beautiful everything must be intelligible' 'Knowledge is virtue.'" From this influence, Nietzsche says that "Euripides measured all the separate elements of the drama—language, characters, dramaturgic structure, and choric music—and corrected them according to these principles."

As an example, Nietzsche cites the addition of the prologue which he describes as a single person who appeared on stage "at the outset of the play, telling us who he is, what precedes the action, what has happened so far, even what will happen in the course of the play." Nietzsche asks, "We know everything that is going to happen; who would want to wait till it actually does happen?"

He points out that this and other additions are based on the false assumption that

> So long as the spectator has to figure out the meaning of this or that person, or the presuppositions of this or that conflict of inclinations and purposes, he cannot become completely absorbed in the activities and sufferings of the chief characters or feel breathless pity and fear.

Nietzsche talks about the necessary creation of a new art form—the Platonic dialogue, which he calls "a mixture of all extant styles and forms, [that] hovers midway between narrative, lyric, and drama, between prose and poetry." Nietzsche condemns the effects of the emphasis on the knowledge and the dialectical format of the new art form:

> For now the virtuous hero must be a dialectician; now there must be a necessary, visible connection between virtue and knowledge, faith and morality; now the transcendental justice of Aeschylus is degraded to the superficial and insolent principle of "poetic" justice with its customary *deus ex machine*.

From Socrates to Science

Nietzsche next traces the quest for knowledge to science. He criticizes the illusion of knowledge:

The profound *illusion* that first saw the light of the world in the person of Socrates: the unshakable faith that thought, using the thread of causality, can penetrate the deepest abysses of being, and that thought is capable not only of knowing being but even of *correcting* it.

He writes about Socrates going freely to his death and the effect that act had:

Hence the image of the *dying Socrates,* as the human being whom knowledge and reason have liberated from the fear of death, is the emblem that, above the entrance gate of science, reminds all of its mission—namely, to make existence appear comprehensible and thus justified; and if reasons do not suffice, *myth* has to come to their aid in the end—myth which I have just called the necessary consequence indeed the purpose of science.

From myth, Nietzsche moves to art, summing up that this "leads science again and again to its limits at which it must turn into *art—which is really the aim of this mechanism.*"

He then stresses the impact this view has had on history and philosophy since:

Once we clearly see how after Socrates, the mystagogue of science, one philosophical school succeeds another, wave upon wave; how the hunger for knowledge reached a never-suspected universality in the widest domain of the educated world, became the real task for every person of higher gifts, and led science onto the high seas from which it has never again been driven altogether.

Music and the Recanted Rebirth

In addition to these arguments, the importance of music also is a key theme throughout *The Birth of Tragedy.* Nietzsche starts off by saying *"Melody is therefore primary and universal."* He discusses the limitations of language: "language is strained to its utmost that it may *imitate music.*" He also says that "the spirit of music just as music itself in its absolute sovereignty does not *need* the image and the concept, but merely *endures* them as accompaniments."

Nietzsche also sees music as best represented by the Dionysian spirit: "The Dionysian spirit in music makes us realize that everything that is born must be prepared to face its painful dissolution. It forces us to gaze into the horror of individual existence, yet without being turned to stone by the vision."

Nietzsche also predicts a rebirth of tragedy in German music, particularly through the works of German composer Richard Wagner, in the remaining sections of *The Birth of Tragedy*. Later when he critiques this work, he will regret these additions. Critics also point out that from Section 15 on, the book's quality deteriorates.

Influence of Schopenhauer, Wagner, and Others

One of the key elements of *The Birth of Tragedy* is the influence of other philosophers, poets, and musicians on this first of Nietzsche's work. As one example, Nietzsche was greatly influenced by Schopenhauer, and he references Schopenhauer's thoughts on will and music. Schopenhauer held that "music is distinguished from all the other arts by the fact that it is not a copy of the phenomenon . . . but a direct copy of the will itself." Nietzsche did not agree entirely; he thought that music could not be will, "but it *appears* as will." Nietzsche also criticized Schopenhauer's description of subject and will, equating his description to "the weird image of the fairy tale which can turn its eyes at will and behold itself; he is at once subject and object, at once poet, actor, and spectator."

Nietzsche also expounds on the poet Schiller's definition of the chorus "as a living wall that tragedy constructs around itself in order to close itself off from the world of reality and to preserve its ideal domain and its poetic freedom." Nietzsche jumps on Lessing's statement that he cared more for the search after truth than truth itself, stating that this statement "thus revealed the fundamental secret of science, to the astonishment, and indeed the anger, of the scientific community." He uses this idea to connect art to science.

What Nietzsche Says in His Criticism of The Birth of Tragedy

One of the best parts of *The Birth of Tragedy* is Nietzsche's own insightful criticism of his work. He states what his goals were, provides a criticism of parts of the work, and underlines how themes in this work are reflected in his life-affirming philosophy. This section talks about this element of *The Birth of Tragedy.*

His Questions

Nietzsche, as mentioned earlier, described some of the questions he sought to answer in this work. In addition to those cited previously, Nietzsche also asked whether the Greeks "ever stronger *craving for beauty,* for festivals, pleasures, new cults was rooted in some deficiency, privation, melancholy pain?" He then ponders the reverse:

> . . . the *craving for the ugly;* the good, severe will of the older Greeks to pessimism, to the tragic myth, to the image of everything underlying existence that is frightful, evil, a riddle, destructive, fatal? What, then, would be the origin of tragedy? Perhaps *joy,* strength, overflowing health, overgreat fullness?

He asks, "Are there perhaps—a question for psychiatrists—neuroses of *health?*" Nietzsche uses the subtitle *Or Hellenism and Pessimism* on the version of *The Birth of Tragedy* with the critique, stressing his contemplation on the role of pessimism.

He wonders whether "the triumph of *optimism,* the gradual prevalence of *rationality,* practical and theoretical *utilitarianism* . . . might have been symptoms of a decline of strength, of impending old age, and of physiological weariness?"

The Effect of His Mentors

Nietzsche also talked about his lack of courage when writing this work, saying it lacked an "individual language" and was instead "expressed by means of Schopenhauerian and Kantian formulas." He provides an insight into how he sees himself when he describes "a spirit with strange, still nameless needs, a memory bursting with questions, experiences, concealed things."

He also criticized the ending of the work saying that he

> . . . appended hope where there was no ground for hope, where everything pointed all too plainly to an end! That on the basis of the latest German music I began to rave about "the German spirit" as if that were in the process even then of discovering and finding itself again.

He adds that he has "learned to consider this 'German spirit' with a sufficient lack of hope or mercy."

His Criticism of Christianity

Nietzsche also gives a great overview of his criticism of Christianity. Within the main sections of *The Birth of Tragedy*, he talks about how myth (or religion) is ritualized and becomes stagnant and problematic:

> For this is the way in which religions are wont to die out: under the stern, intelligent eyes of an orthodox dogmatism, the mythical premises of a religion are systematized as a sum total of historical events; one begins apprehensively to defend the credibility of the myths, while at the same time one opposes any continuation of their natural vitality and growth; the feeling for myth perishes, and its place is taken by the claim of religion to historical foundations.

About Christianity, he writes:

> Christianity was from the beginning, essentially and fundamentally, life's nausea and disgust with life, merely concealed behind, masked by, dressed up as, faith in 'another' or 'better' life. Hatred of 'the world,' condemnations of the passions, fear of beauty and sensuality, a beyond invented the better to slander this life, at bottom a craving for the nothing, for the end, for respite.

He shows how this emphasis affects life, promoting an anti-life view:

> For confronted with morality . . . life *must* continually and inevitably be in the wrong, because life *is* something essentially amoral—and eventually, crushed by the weight of contempt and eternal No, life *must* then be felt to be worthy of desire and altogether worthless. . . . Might not morality be 'a will to negate life,' a secret instinct of annihilation, a principle of decay, diminution, and slander—the beginning of the end?

His Life View

From these criticisms, Nietzsche forms his own life philosophy, and he describes it this way:

It was *against* morality that my instinct turned with this questionable book, long ago; it was an instinct that aligned itself with life and that discovered for itself a fundamentally opposite doctrine and valuation of life—purely artistic and *anti-Christian* . . . I called it Dionysian.

Instead he recommends that "you ought to learn the art of *this-worldly comfort first;* you ought to learn to laugh." Nietzsche always stresses the importance of laughter and details his issues with a wide variety of topics.

4 The Gay Science

*What makes us heroic?—Confronting
simultaneously our supreme suffering
and our supreme hope.*
—Nietzsche, *The Gay Science*

In his early writings, Nietzsche wrote essays (as in *The Birth of Tragedy*), but mid-career he turned to a new style of writing, penning *aphorisms,* short sections of prose, each with its own insight. The first work published in this format was *Human, All-Too-Human* (1878), but probably his best-known work in this format was *The Gay Science* (1882). This work introduced so many of Nietzsche's themes, themes that he would continue to address in his many other works.

In his introduction to *The Portable Nietzsche,* Walter Kaufmann, noted scholar, editor, and translator of Nietzsche's works, calls *The Gay Science* "a storehouse of treasures that contains some of Nietzsche's most sustained treatments of important epistemological questions as well as some of his most profound observations about art and ethics." This chapter introduces this work and explains the significance of the title, its structure, and its key themes.

The Gay Science Defined

It's easy to mistake *The Gay Science* for something it's not because of its title and because of the short seemingly miscellaneous structure of the aphorisms. To start, consider what Nietzsche meant by the title and also the careful planning and arrangement of the contents of this work.

Note that the meaning of *gay* is different today than it was when Nietzsche wrote the work, so the title can be misinterpreted. Sometimes the title of this work is translated as *The Joyous Science* to avoid any misunderstanding.

What Is Gay Science?

One of the main ideas that Nietzsche presents is that knowledge, especially science, should not be taken too seriously, but should be approached with a joyous and happy attitude. Nietzsche says "'where laughter and gaiety are found, thinking does not amount to anything': that is the prejudice of the serious beast against all 'gay science.'—Well then, let us prove this is a prejudice."

The name of this work underlines this main concept. Science (and by this Nietzsche means any learning or knowledge) does not have to be so serious. Nietzsche deals with many of the myths (including its seriousness) of knowledge in *The Gay Science*. Nietzsche is not *against* science; he is opposed to the whole philosophical tradition where reason dominates emotion and other potential ways to knowledge. He seeks to illuminate and challenge the prevailing attitudes about science. Instead of science removed from life, he seeks a science that is relevant. Instead of a blind acceptance of what is supposed to be true, he advocates questioning and seeking the truth as an individual quest. He promotes an approach to knowledge that celebrates learning, embraces experiments, and accepts mistakes.

Structure

The Gay Science consists of five books, and each book is comprised of aphorisms that are anywhere from one sentence to several paragraphs in length. Each aphorism has a title and number. If you pick up *The Gay Science* and look through it, the contents may appear as a series of short, off-the-cuff remarks that are not related, but this is misleading.

First, the brevity of the aphorism belies the depth and insight it provides. As an example, consider this short statement: "We hear only those questions for which we are in a position to find answers." It's short, yet clever and wise, giving the reader something to ponder. Nietzsche talked about his intent with this writing style. He writes, "In the mountains the shortest route is from peak to peak, but for that you must have long legs. Aphorisms should be peaks: and those to whom they are spoken should be big and tall of stature." It's much more difficult to say a lot with fewer words!

Second, the contents may appear to be random and unrelated. This is another mistake. Not only are the ideas presented all interconnected, but

Nietzsche also circles back to these same ideas in other works. All of Nietzsche's writings are interrelated, and most misunderstandings of Nietzsche's writings occur when a particular thought or quotation is taken out of context.

If you read closely, you'll see the threads of the work interwoven, and you'll note the importance of the placement of each aphorism. As just one example, Nietzsche ends Book II with "And as long as you are in any way *ashamed* before yourselves, you do not yet belong with us." This same idea is echoed at the end of Book III: "What is the seal of liberation—No longer being ashamed in front of oneself." Part of the challenge in reading Nietzsche is seeing the part as it relates to the whole.

The Importance of The Gay Science

Nietzsche uses this unique writing style in *The Gay Science* to present many of his key themes, concepts that he will return to and elaborate on in other works. In particular, this work is where Nietzsche famously wrote "God is dead." He also introduces the concept of eternal recurrence, superman (or overman), and the will to power. The character *Zarathustra,* from his next work *Thus Spoke Zarathustra,* makes an appearance in *The Gay Science.* (Nietzsche worked on *Thus Spoke Zarathustra* in the middle of writing *The Gay Science.*)

In addition, Nietzsche addresses the theme of knowledge; discusses the influence of other philosophers, writers, and artists—including Wagner, Schopenhauer, Emerson, Socrates, and Shakespeare—on his work; develops a criticism of how morals are created and sustained; and covers many other topics, from women to art, from friendship to death. The rest of this chapter highlights some of the key themes of this work.

The Myths of Knowledge

As mentioned, the title underlines one of the key themes in *The Gay Science:* knowledge. Nietzsche talks about how it is acquired, why it is important, how it has been developed, what approaches have been taken, and more. He challenges his reader to look closely at these various aspects, starting with the goal of knowledge.

Why Knowledge?

Nietzsche asks his reader to consider the usefulness of existing knowledge. He points out some of the drawbacks of existing knowledge saying, "We cannot even reproduce our thoughts entirely in words." He says that science's current importance is due to three errors:

> . . . science has been promoted, partly because it was by means of science that one hoped to understand God's goodness and wisdom best . . . partly because one believed in the absolute utility of knowledge, and especially in the most intimate association of morality, knowledge, and happiness . . . partly because one thought that in science one possessed and loved something unselfish, harmless, self-sufficient, and truly innocent, in which man's evil impulse had no part whatever.

This aphorism is aptly titled "Owing to three errors." In addition, he challenges the reader to look at the history and origins of science:

> Do you really believe that the sciences would ever have originated and grown if the way had not been prepared by magicians, alchemists, astrologers, and witches whose promises and pretensions first had to create a thirst, a hunger, a taste for *hidden* and *forbidden* powers?

By seeing the underlying goal or motive of science, the reader understands how science became so esteemed, so serious.

Question the "Truth"

Nietzsche also gets readers to see that what they *think* they know may not be actually what they *do* know. He basically says that science may currently provide better descriptions, but it still does not provide explanations. Why? Because an explanation is never possible. He writes that "'Explanation' is what we call it, but it is 'description' that distinguishes us from older stages of knowledge and science . . . nobody has explained a push."

He questions man's desire to see meaning in all things and writes that the universe is "neither perfect nor beautiful, nor noble, nor does it wish to become any of these things; it does not by any means strive to imitate man." He continues, cautioning the reader to "beware of saying there are laws in nature. There are only necessities: there is no one to command, no one to obey, no one to transgress."

Whose Truth?

Nietzsche tells his readers not to be followers, but to find their own truth. He shows how people willingly follow what others say and do (or *say* to say and do) without much thought:

The great majority of people does not consider it contemptible to believe this or that and to live accordingly without first having given themselves an account of the final and most certain reasons pro and con, and without even troubling themselves about such reasons afterward.

Nietzsche no longer lets the readers hide in what the majority thinks. And if they do so, he makes them at least aware that they are going along with something without any real reasons of their own.

Knowledge of What?

Continuing his critique, Nietzsche asks his reader to consider what type of knowledge is relevant to his or her life. To Nietzsche, self-knowledge is the most important, and he stresses this when he questions, "Where is there a history of love, avarice, envy, conscience, piety, cruelty?" He continues:

Has anyone made a study of the different ways of dividing up the day or the consequences of a regular schedule of work, festivals, and rest? What is known of the moral effects of different foods? Is there any philosophy of nutrition. . . . Has the dialectic of marriage and friendship ever been explicated?

Nietzsche advocates that his readers evaluate knowledge and its truth. He points out how easily one is deceived:

Whoever knows he is deep tries to be clear, but whoever wants to seem deep to the crowd tries to be obscure. For the crowd supposes that anything it cannot see to the bottom must be deep: it is so timid and goes so unwillingly into the water.

No more is Nietzsche's criticism of what is accepted as knowledge or "truth" more apparent than when the reader considers the concept of God.

Where Is God?

The Gay Science is where Nietzsche first says that "God is dead." The madman searching for God says:

We have killed him—you and I. All of us are his murderers. But how did we do this? How could we drink up the sea? Who gave us the sponge to wipe away the entire horizon? What were we doing when we unchained this earth from its sun? . . . Do we hear nothing as yet of the noise of

the gravediggers who are burying God? . . . How shall we comfort ourselves, the murderers of all murderers?

Instead of feeling despair or being afraid in a godless world, Nietzsche
finds this news hopeful. He writes

Indeed, we philosophers and "free spirits" feel, when we hear the news
that "the old god is dead," as if a new dawn shown on us; our heart overflows with gratitude, amazement, premonitions, expectations. At long
last the horizon appears free to us again.

Nietzsche objects to the reliance on religion to tell one how to live and
what is good and bad. He says, "The Christian resolution to find the world
ugly and bad has made the world ugly and bad." He calls liquor and Christianity the "European narcotics." He objects to Christianity's denial of all
that is of this world, of living for the next life, which Nietzsche does not
believe exists.

Nietzsche knows how entrenched this view of the world is and how difficult it will be to change to a different way of thinking. He says

After Buddha was dead, his shadow was still shown for centuries in a
cave—a tremendous, gruesome shadow. God is dead; but given the way
of men, there will still be caves for thousands of years in which his shadow
will be shown. And we—we still have to vanquish his shadow too.

To "vanquish his shadow," Nietzsche challenges his readers to consider
current morals and concepts of what is good and evil. He urges his readers
to trace how morality is developed and see the flaws in the existing
philosophy.

Whose Morality?

Nietzsche questions the concept of evil (especially as it relates to life on earth
versus life in heaven). He says that anything that challenges the existing
thought is considered bad or evil. He writes, "What is new, however, is
always *evil*, being that which wants to conquer and overthrow the old
boundary markers and the old pieties; and only what is old is good."

He also questions the assumptions of "good" promoting man's evolution and "bad" deterring that development. He offers that things that
are considered "bad" actually initiate changes and promote growth:

One holds that what is called good preserves the species, while what is called evil harms the species. In truth, however, the evil instincts are expedient, species-preserving, and indispensable to as high a degree as the good ones; their function is merely different.

He brings this idea close to the reader when he challenges him to consider who benefits from so-called "good" virtues. He says

A man's virtues are called *good* depending on their probable consequences not for him but for us and society. . . . Otherwise one would have had to notice that virtues (like industriousness, obedience, chastity, filial piety, and justice) are usually harmful for those who possess them.

He continues this idea showing how these virtues are continued and upheld:

That is how education always proceeds: one tries to condition an individual by various attractions and advantages to adopt a way of thinking and behaving that, once it has become a habit, instinct, and passion, will dominate him *to his own ultimate disadvantage* but "for the general good."

He particularly singles out pity as harmful because no one can really understand another's misery and pretending to do so comforts the person who feels the pity, not the person who is in pain. He also associates pity (as well as guilt) with Christianity. He says

But whenever people *notice* that we suffer, they interpret our suffering superficially. It is the very essence of the emotion of pity that it strips away from the suffering of others whatever is distinctively personal . . . one simply knows nothing of the whole inner sequence and intricacies that are distress for *me* or for *you*.

Nietzsche offers a different version of what is good or noble; he defines *noble* as "the discovery of values for which no scale has been invented yet offering sacrifices on alters that are dedicated to an unknown god; a courage without desire for honors; a self-sufficiency that overflows and gives to men and things." He says that he wants to teach "what is understood by so few today, least of all by these preachers of pity: *to share not suffering but joy.*" To that effect, he provides his own view of a purposeful life.

What Purpose Life?

Rather than look to someone else (or religion or science) to tell someone how to live, Nietzsche advises his readers to look within and to participate fully in this life, here on earth. Some of Nietzsche's most life-affirming statements occur in *The Gay Science;* it is this work where he defines *amor fati,* advises his readers to live dangerously, and stresses the individual rather than the crowd (or herd). This section discusses this aspect of his philosophy.

Love This Life

Many readers have mistaken Nietzsche for a pessimistic philosopher, in part because he denies God but also because of his association with Schopenhauer, who was pessimistic. How can one live happily in a life that has no ultimate purpose? Nietzsche provides much to consider on just that question.

Nietzsche stresses finding satisfaction from within rather than from outside: "For one thing is needful: that a human being should *attain* satisfaction with himself, whether it be by means of this or that poetry and art; only then is a human being at all tolerable to behold." Resentment occurs when a person is unable to accept himself; Nietzsche says, "Whoever is dissatisfied with himself is continually ready for revenge, and we others will be his victims."

As mentioned in Chapter 2, Nietzsche describes how to "give style to one's character." And to do so, he says that he wants "to learn more and more to see as beautiful what is necessary in things; then I shall be one of those who makes things beautiful." (He goes on to describe *amor fati*—"love of fate"—in this same passage, also referenced in Chapter 2.) Anyone who found Nietzsche pessimistic would have to ignore his wish to "all in all and on the whole: I want someday to be purely and simply a Yes-sayer!" as well as his encouragement to live dangerously:

> For believe me!—the secret to harvesting the greatest abundance and the greatest enjoyment from existence is this—living dangerously! Build your cities on the slopes of Vesuvius! Send your ships into uncharted seas! Live at war with your peers and yourselves! Be robbers and conquerors, so long as you cannot be rulers and possessors, you knowing ones! The time will soon be past when you could be content to live hidden in the forests like timid deer.

Be an Individual

Throughout his work, Nietzsche stresses the individual. (The philosophy that stresses the individual is known as *Existentialism,* and many of Nietzsche's themes make him a philosopher who greatly influenced the creation and formation of this philosophy. Note that Nietzsche didn't use that term, and he should not be pigeon-holed as a specific "type" of philosopher.) In one short passage, he stresses the importance of the individual. He asks, "What does your conscience say?" and then answers, "You must become who it is that you are."

In the process of becoming, Nietzsche does not want individuals to hide or feel shame for any mistakes. He doesn't believe that absolute truth is possible anyway. Therefore, he advises his readers to accept and embrace their mistakes. He writes that a thinker should not feel remorse over mistakes if the thinker "sees his own actions as experiments and questions—as attempts to find out something. Success and failure are for him *answers* above all." He proclaims "on the whole I do not know whether I do not have more reason to be grateful to my failures than to my successes."

Laugh!

In being willing to make mistakes and accepting them, Nietzsche recommends having a good sense of humor. Throughout his writing, he stresses the importance of laughter and humor. In his writing, he is anything but dry, dull, or preachy. He was, in fact, funny. He writes

> We must discover the *hero* no less than the *fool* in our passion for knowledge; we must occasionally find pleasure in our folly, or we cannot continue to find pleasure in our wisdom . . . we need all exuberant, floating, dancing, mocking, childish, and blissful art les we lose the *freedom above things* that our ideal demands of us."

Consider this passage as a summary of the importance of humor:

> . . . life has not disappointed me. On the contrary, I find it truer, more desirable and mysterious every year—ever since the day when the great liberator came to me: the idea that life could be an experiment of the seeker for knowledge—and not a duty, not a calamity, not trickery. . . . *"Life as a means to knowledge"*—with this principle in one's heart one can live not only boldly but even gaily, and laugh gaily, too.

What Else?

So far, this chapter has highlighted Nietzsche's criticism of knowledge, science, God, and existing morals, as well as his concepts for a different approach to life. In addition to these key themes, Nietzsche also introduces some important ideas. These are ideas that he continues to address in books to follow. In particular, *The Gay Science* introduces:

- **Will to power:** Nietzsche says that "The great and small struggle always revolves around superiority, around growth and expansion, around power—in accordance with the will to power which is the will of life."

- **Superman:** Nietzsche describes the evolution of man and creates the idea of the "superman" (also translated as the "overman"). He views this ideal as an individual, not part of the crowd. He writes, "It was here that the luxury of the individuals was first permitted; it was here that one first honored the rights of individuals. The invention of gods, heroes, and supermen of all kinds."

- **Eternal recurrence:** The idea of living the same life over and over is introduced in *The Gay Science.* He asks the reader to consider his reaction to the statements that

"This life as you now live it and have lived it, you will have to live once more and innumerable times more; and there will be nothing new in it, but every pain and every joy and every thought and sigh and everything immeasurably small or great in your life must return to you—all in the same succession and sequence."

Starting with a reaction of fear and despair, Nietzsche later shows how to transform these into other possibilities, including embracing the idea of the same life over and over.

Other chapters in this book address these themes in more detail. In addition, this chapter only touches on *some* of the main ideas; the work is full of many other topics including thoughts on women, art, poetry, and friendship. What Nietzsche says, for instance, about women runs the gamut from stereotypical to enlightening. As just one example, Nietzsche wrote about how women change themselves to fit the ideal that men hold of them: "For it is man who creates for himself the image of woman, and woman forms herself according to this image."

The Gay Science also offers Nietzsche's criticism of German music and language. Anyone who thinks that Nietzsche was a Nazi and promoted German nationalism would do well to read all that he says about Germans. He also assesses both the strengths and weakness of two individuals who were important to his development: Wagner (disparaging in particular his vanity) and Schopenhauer (Nietzsche criticizes his "unprovable doctrine of the One Will," "the denial of the individual," and "the nonsense about pity"). He talks about how the love of freedom may require that one "be capable of sacrificing one's dearest friend for it" much as he did when he moved away from these influences and came into his own.

5 Thus Spoke Zarathustra

In heaven all the interesting people are missing.

—Nietzsche

Thus Spoke Zarathustra was Nietzsche's most popular and best-known work. He wrote the first part in just ten days. Noted translator and Nietzsche scholar, Walter Kaufmann says in his Introduction to this work in *The Portable Nietzsche,* "[T]here are few works to match its wealth of ideas, the abundance of profound suggestions, the epigrams, the wit." This chapter discusses the structure, style, and themes of this work.

An Introduction to Thus Spoke Zarathustra

Thus Spoke Zarathustra was first published in 1883, and this book is a work of fiction, a difference from Nietzsche's earlier writing styles. The fourth part was added in 1885; Nietzsche could not find a publisher for this part, so he paid for the publication of forty copies but could barely find ten people to which to send copies.

This section discusses the fictional character Zarathustra and the organization of this work as well as provides an overview of the key themes introduced in it.

Who Is Zarathustra?

Zarathustra or Zoroaster was a great Persian prophet (629–551 B.C.). He founded the religion Zendavesta, which is still practiced today in some parts of India and was the religion of Persia before Islam. In *Thus Spoke Zarathustra,* Zarathustra is a lonely, wise wanderer. No one understands him or wants to listen to him. Most critics agree that Zarathustra is a fictional version of Nietzsche. When Zarathustra speaks, Nietzsche is speaking through him.

How Thus Spoke Zarathustra Is Organized

The complete work *Thus Spoke Zarathustra* consists of four parts, each with sixteen to twenty-two sections. The sections of the first three parts are self-contained. In the last part, the sections tell one story. Each section has its own title, and the titles provide the topic for that passage (for instance, "On Love of the Neighbor" or "On the Three Evils").

The work begins with a Prologue that provides the story of Zarathustra. When he was thirty years old, Zarathustra left his home and went to live in the mountains. He lived there for ten years with his companions—an eagle and a serpent. He finally tells the sun, "I am weary of my wisdom, like a bee that has gathered too much honey; I need hands outstretched to receive it." He decides to leave the mountain: "I must *go under*—go down, as it is said by man, to whom I want to descend." The rest of the work tells of his journey and those he meets along the way.

The Prologue, like much of Nietzsche's work, is full of allusions to both the Bible and classical works. For instance, the opening prologue has many similarities to the story of Jesus and Plato's Myth of the Cave.

Nietzsche also loved plays on words, and he included many of these in his work. Sometimes translations are unable to do justice to his command of the language. Modern readers may miss out on some of the richness of the work because they don't catch all the references to other works and all the poetry and playfulness of the wording.

Key Themes in Thus Spoke Zarathustra

Thus Spoke Zarathustra was published after *The Gay Science,* and this work continues the themes discussed in that earlier work. In particular, the following themes are discussed and elaborated on:

- **The evolution of man:** Nietzsche criticizes the current state of man and predicts how man will end up if he stays on this course. As an alternative, he offers his "superman" or "overman." *Thus Spoke Zarathustra* is the work that describes in most detail this concept.

- **A life with meaning:** The meaning of life isn't found in another life (heaven) but is found here on earth, and it's up to man to give meaning to his life. In doing so, he wills his own existence and creates his own values.

- **Eternal recurrence:** First introduced in *The Gay Science,* Nietzsche's attitude toward this principle of the same life over and over again changes from horror to acceptance to joy.

The rest of this chapter discusses these themes as well as other points of interest found in *Thus Spoke Zarathustra.*

It's Superman!

Nietzsche describes mankind this way: "Mankind is a rope tied between beast and superman—a rope over an abyss." Through Zarathustra, Nietzsche presents a criticism of man as he currently exists. He views man as overly concerned with comforts, with wanting things easy, with not questioning things too deeply. He describes him as petty and small. He sees this path leading to the "last man," whom Nietzsche also describes.

In contrast to these pictures, Nietzsche presents another possibility, *Ubermensch,* translated as "superman" or "overman." Nietzsche presents the superman as an ideal, not necessarily a given. He presents this man as something—in a life without any given meaning—to strive for. These stages are not evolution in the biological sense, but are psychological possibilities, a way of living or striving to live.

Throughout the parts of *Thus Spoke Zarathustra,* the reader gets a good idea of the various "evolutionary" possibilities.

Heading toward the "Last Man"

Nietzsche describes his vision of the last man. In this vision, "Everybody wants the same, everybody is the same: whoever feels different goes voluntarily into a madhouse." This man is indifferent and fears anything that is different. His views might best be summed up by the soothsayer that appears in Part 4: "All is the same, nothing is worth while, the world is without meaning, knowledge strangles."

Nietzsche describes how these men claimed to have "placed our chair in the middle"; Nietzsche says this "is mediocrity, though it be called moderation." He says, "Thus they try to please and gratify everybody. This, however, is cowardice, even if it be called virtue."

He says that the last man asks, "'What is love? What is creation? What is longing? What is a star?'" He writes that "[t]he earth has become small, and on it hops the last man, who makes everything small. His race is as ineradicable as the flea-beetle; the last man lives the longest."

Nietzsche says, "I have seen them both naked, the greatest and the smallest men:—and they are still all-too-similar to one another. Verily, even the greatest I found to be—all-too-human." But he offers a new version. He proclaims, "I will teach men the meaning of their existence—the overman, the lightning out of the dark cloud of man."

Striving toward Superman

From the current state of apathy and fear-based living, Nietzsche presents a different goal. He presents the superman, and he offers superman as an ideal, as a goal. He says, "'The time has come for man to set himself a goal. The time has come for man to plant the seed of his highest hope.'"

That highest hope is superman, and the goal is to overcome man: "I teach you the superman. Man is something to be overcome. What have you done to overcome him?" Nietzsche thinks there is a lot in man that must be overcome or changed, much that is polluted. But he believes that this is possible: "Verily, a polluted stream is man. One must actually be a sea to take in a polluted stream without becoming impure. Behold, I teach you the superman: he is this sea, in him can your great contempt go under."

Nietzsche says that "The 'overcoming' of man is in fact the overcoming of oneself." He means that man must overcome his own fears, and he must realize his own values and meaning. He must recognize his own power to create.

Nietzsche also thinks that striving toward this ideal can provide meaning to one's life. He writes:

> The superman is the meaning of the earth. Let your will say: the superman is to be the meaning of the earth! I beseech you, my brothers, be true to the earth, and do not believe those who speak to you of other-worldly hopes! They are poisoners, whether they know it or not.

In Part 4, Nietzsche provides some of the qualities of this superman. He says that he must be brave: "Brave is he who knows fear but *conquers* fear, who sees the abyss, but with *pride*." He must be honest and rely on himself. Nietzsche writes, "If you would go high, use your own legs. Do not let yourselves be *carried* up; do not sit on the backs and heads of others."

Other concepts in *Thus Spoke Zarathustra,* such as creating meaning on earth, relate to this ideal of superman. The rest of this chapter covers these additional components of this ideal.

Finding Meaning

Nietzsche urges his readers to find meaning in life now, rather than invest belief in some other life. He equates preachers of "eternal life" with preachers of death and explains how this becomes appealing:

> And you, too, for whom life is furious work and unrest—are you not very weary of life? Are you not very ripe for the preaching of death? . . . you find it hard to bear yourselves; your industry is escape and the will to forget yourselves. If you believed more in life you would fling yourselves less to the moment. But you do not have contents enough in yourselves for waiting—and not even for idleness.

He says that the afterworld was created by those who despise the body and earth. They "hate the lover of knowledge and that youngest among the virtues which is called 'honesty.'" Instead, he advises his readers to listen "to the voice of the healthy body . . . it speaks of the meaning of the earth."

Nietzsche urges his readers to wake up and realize the missed opportunity. He casts this lost opportunity in religious language—as sin:

> Once the sin against God was the greatest sin, but God died, and so these sinners died as well. To sin against the earth is now the most terrible thing, and to esteem the entrails of the unknowable more highly than the meaning of the earth.

He calls his readers to invest in this life, to find meaning in this earthy life. He writes, "No longer to bury one's head in the sand of heavenly things, but to bear it freely, an earthly head, which creates a meaning for the earth." In creating meaning, he shows how man becomes his own creator and creates meaning and value.

Your Will

Instead of looking to an outside source, Nietzsche wants man to see himself as a creator. Rather than give his power away to some other source, he urges man to claim his power and use it to create. Nietzsche borrows this idea from Schopenhauer, but removes the pessimism. He shows how man creates value and has always been the creator of any value, in particular moral value:

> Men gave themselves all their good and evil. Verily, they did not take it, they did not find it, nor did it come as a voice from heaven. Only man placed values in things to preserve himself—he alone created a meaning for things, a human meaning. Therefore he calls himself "man," which means: the esteemer.

Nietzsche next equates *esteem* with *create*. He says "Creation—that is the great redemption from suffering, and life's growing light." He wants his readers to consider the power of his will. He writes, "Whatever in me has feeling, suffers and is in prison; but my will always comes to me as my liberator and joy-bringer. Willing liberates: that is the true teaching of will and liberty." He explains how this will leads away from God toward man: "Away from God and gods this will has lured me; what could one create if gods existed? But my fervent will to create impels me ever again toward man."

Nietzsche explains what man can do with this will and what it means: "This is what the will to truth should mean to you: that everything be changed into what is thinkable for man, visible for man, feelable by man. You should think through your own senses to their consequences." Not only that, but he shows the connection between will, creation, and truth: "And what you have called world, that shall be created only by you: your reason, your image, your will, your love shall thus be realized."

Your Virtues

One of Nietzsche's main criticisms of Christianity was its emphasis on punishment and suffering and the promise for a future reward. Is someone pure of heart if her motive is really based on receiving a reward or avoiding punishment? Nietzsche wants his readers to see the flawed thinking. Of the promised reward, he writes:

> You who are virtuous still want to be paid! Do you want rewards for virtue, and heaven for earth, and the eternal for today? And now are you angry with me because I teach there is no reward and paymaster? And verily, I do not even teach that virtue is its own reward . . . they have lied reward and punishment into the foundation of things.

Nietzsche wants his readers to see that they are "too *pure* for the filth of the words: revenge, punishment, reward, retribution."

He shows the connection of punishment with the desire for revenge: "*The spirit of revenge,* my friends has so far been the subject of man's best reflection; and where there was suffering, one always wanted punishment too. For 'punishment' is what revenge calls itself."

Nietzsche tells man to create and honor his own values, not those that someone else gave to him. Nietzsche explains how unwanted things weigh down a man:

> Life is a grave burden. But only man is a grave burden for himself! That is because he carries on his shoulders too much that is alien to him. Like a camel, he kneels down and lets himself be well loaded . . . he loads too many *alien* grave words and values on himself, and then life seems a desert to him.

In Part 4, when summarizing the qualities of the superman, Nietzsche cautions against doing things "for" someone else. Nietzsche says "Unlearn this 'for.'" He writes that "Your work, your will, that is *your* 'neighbor': do not let yourselves be gulled with false values!"

Your Own Way

Nietzsche, then, advises man to create a life on earth with its own meaning and with values that are meaningful and valid to him. In doing so, that person has to look within and discover what he values, and Nietzsche acknowledges this process isn't easy. He says, "Man is hard to discover—hardest of all for himself."

He explains that self-knowledge and creation is a process. He describes it this way: "[H]e who would learn to fly one day must first learn to stand and walk and run and climb and dance: one cannot fly into flying." He explains that he reached his own truth not by following but by trying things for himself. He says, "I reached my own truth: it was not on one ladder that I climbed to the height where my eye roams over my distance. And it was only reluctantly that I ever inquired about the way . . . I preferred to question and try out the ways themselves."

He acknowledges the role of mistakes and urges his readers to embrace and celebrate the mistakes. (Another thing about Christianity that Nietzsche dislikes is the idea that if you make a mistake you suffer punishment, maybe even eternal damnation. You must pray for mercy.) He reminds his readers, "[H]ave you not all failed?" and says that "all good things approach their goal crookedly." He recommends laughter: "Be of good cheer, what does it matter? How much is still possible! Learn to laugh at yourselves as one must laugh!" Throughout his work, Nietzsche stresses the importance of laughter: "This crown to crown the laughing man, this rose-wreath crown: I myself have set this crown upon my head, I myself have pronounced my laughter holy."

Zarathustra does not want disciples. Instead he urges, "I bid you lose me and find yourselves." In the end, he reminds his readers that there is no one way; that each person must find his own way. He says, "This is *my* way; where is yours?—this I answered those who asked me 'the way.' For *the* way—that does not exist." He says, "Become who you are!"

Life Again and Again

In *The Gay Science,* Nietzsche introduces the idea of eternal recurrence, and this idea nauseates him. This idea has one living the same life over and over again. Nietzsche argues the logic of this, posed at the intersection of two paths, at the spot marked "The Moment":

> Must not whatever *can* walk have walked on this lane before? Must not whatever *can* happen have happened, have been done, have passed by before? . . . must not all of us have been there before? . . . And return and walk in that other lane, out there, before us, in this long dreadful lane—must we not eternally return?

He repeats this same idea later:

> Everything goes, everything comes back; eternally rolls the wheel of being. Everything dies, everything blossoms again; eternally runs the year of being. Everything breaks, everything is joined anew; eternally the same house of being is built. Everything parts, everything greets every other thing again; eternally the ring of being remains faithful to itself. In every Now, being begins; round every Here rolls the sphere There. The center is everywhere. Bent is the path of eternity.

Nietzsche clarifies that it's not a different life, but the same life: "I come again, with this sun, with this earth, with this eagle, with this serpent—*not* to a new life or a better life or a similar life: I come back eternally to this same, selfsame life."

At first, he responds to his thought with nausea ("eternal recurrence . . . that was my disgust with all existence . . . Nausea! Nausea! Nausea!) but the end of Part 3 concludes with "The Seven Seals OR The Yes and Amen Song." Each verse ends with "For I love you, O eternity."

And in Part 4 Nietzsche more dramatically accepts the idea of eternal recurrence. He writes:

> Have you ever said Yes to a single you! O my friends, then you said Yes too to *all* woe. All things are entangled, ensnared, enamored; if ever you wanted one thing twice, if ever you said, "You please me, happiness! Abide, moment!" then you wanted all back. All anew, then you *loved* the world. Eternal ones, love it eternally and evermore; and to woe too, you say: go, but return! *For all joy wants—eternity.*

In *Thus Spoke Zarathustra*, Nietzsche also discusses the idea of the "will to be master." He writes, "He who cannot obey himself will be commanded. Such is the nature of all living things." In *Beyond Good and Evil*, he describes the evolution and evaluation of morals and the concept of will to power in more detail. This work is the topic of the next chapter.

6 Beyond Good and Evil

*Whoever fights monsters should see to it
that in the process he does not become
a monster. And when you look long into
an abyss, the abyss also looks into you.*

—Nietzsche, *Beyond Good and Evil*

Beyond Good and Evil is one of Nietzsche's most important books; he completed this book after *Thus Spoke Zarathustra*, and it discusses Nietzsche's philosophy in a different style. In *The Portable Nietzsche*, Walter Kaufmann says this about the work:

> It is possible to say briefly what makes the book great: the prophetic independence of its spirit; the hundreds of doors it opens for the mind, revealing new vistas, problems, and relationships; and what it contributes to our understanding of much of recent thought and literature and history.

This chapter discusses this work and its main themes.

About Good and Evil

Beyond Good and Evil was published in 1886, after *Thus Spoke Zarathustra*. As mentioned in Chapter 5, *Thus Spoke Zarathustra* is a fictional work; in this style, Nietzsche conveys his themes indirectly (much like a near contemporary of his, Kierkegaard). *Beyond Good and Evil* takes a different approach to presenting the same ideas. In fact, Nietzsche sent a copy of his work to a friend, writing, "it says the same things as my Zarathustra, but differently, very differently" *(The Portable Nietzsche)*. In *Beyond Good and Evil*, Nietzsche addresses his readers directly, in a straightforward style. When he writes that "[i]n a man devoted to knowledge, pity seems almost ridiculous, like delicate hands on a Cyclops," the reader recognizes that his writing, as in all his works, is creative, funny, descriptive, and challenging.

The book is divided into nine parts, each with descriptive subtitles. The parts are divided into short sections, which are meant to be read and taken as a whole. Each section qualifies and builds on what was said previously. In the past, statements have been taken out of context, leading to a misunderstanding of what Nietzsche really said. Readers are cautioned not to do the same, but instead to consider *all* he said about a topic and its context.

Nietzsche's intention with the title is to urge a new philosophy that is beyond good and evil, beyond simple black-and-white thinking. He describes this aim in this passage:

> . . . that without accepting the fictions of logic, without measuring reality against the purely invented world of the unconditional and self-identical, without a constant falsification of the world by means of numbers, many could not live—that renouncing false judgments would mean renouncing life and a denial of life. To recognize untruth as a condition of life—that certainly means resisting accustomed value feelings in a dangerous way; and a philosophy that risks this would by that token alone place itself beyond good and evil.

Like his other works, *Beyond Good and Evil* did not achieve commercial success during Nietzsche's lifetime. He had hoped to sell three hundred copies of the book, but sold less than half that many. Later, of course, the book was quite successful. Nietzsche's themes of a new type of philosopher, his description of morals, and his definition of nobleness are still influential.

Cultivating a New Philosopher

Part 1 of *Beyond Good and Evil,* "On the Prejudices of Philosophers," opens the work with a look at the existing state of philosophy and philosophers. Nietzsche provides a critique of science and knowledge and then offers suggestions for a new type of philosopher. He stresses logic and reason for a useful purpose, rather than abstract. About reason, he says the key question we should ask "is to what extent it is life-promoting, life-preserving, species-preserving, perhaps even species-cultivating." This section describes this element of the work.

The State of Current Philosophers

Nietzsche offers that, in evaluating philosophical thought, one should ask "at what morality does all this (does *he*) aim?" Nietzsche does not believe that the "'drive to knowledge' is the father of philosophy." Instead, he says that "every drive wants to be master—and it attempts to philosophize in *that spirit.*"

He points out that, although the goal is objectivity (conclusions reached by logic and reason), in reality objectivity is not possible. He sums up this dishonesty and the underlying motive:

> They are not honest enough in their work. . . . They all pose as if they had discovered and reached their real opinions through the self-development of a cold, pure, divinely unconcerned dialectic . . . while at bottom it is an assumption, a hunch, indeed a kind of "inspiration"— most often a desire of the heart that has been filtered and made abstract—that they defend with reasons they have sought after the fact.

He continues, stating that "it has been clear to me what every great philosopher so far has been: namely, the personal confession of its author and a kind of involuntary and unconscious memoir."

The Ideal New Philosopher

In lieu of the current assumptions and goals of philosophy, Nietzsche defines and articulates qualities of a "new philosopher." The reader can find qualities of this philosopher particularly in Nietzsche's description of a free spirit and in his analysis of "we scholars."

The new philosopher, according to Nietzsche, is an independent; he is not limited to a person, a fatherland, a pity, a science, to his own detachment or virtues. He hopes that "such a philosopher of the future may perhaps say of himself" that "'[m]y judgment is *my* judgment': no one else is easily entitled to it."

He provides a catalog of the dangers of a philosopher—that the philosopher "grows weary," is "detained somewhere to become a 'specialist,'" or "attains it too late, when his best time and strength are spent." He sums up the dangers and things that must be overcome:

> . . . having escaped again and again from the musty agreeable nooks into which preference and prejudice, youth, origin, the accidents of people and books or even exhaustion from wandering seemed to have banished us; full of malice against the lures of dependence that lie hidden in honors, or money, or offices, or enthusiasms of the senses; grateful even to need and vacillating sickness because they always rid us from some rule

and its "prejudice," . . . investigators to the point of cruelty, . . . ready for every venture.

In addition to these dangers, Nietzsche says that the philosopher has also the demand of a judgment, "not about the sciences but about life and the value of life." And in making this judgment, the philosopher "must seek his way to this right and faith only from the most comprehensive—perhaps most disturbing and destructive—experiences, and frequently hesitates, doubts, and lapses into silence."

To Nietzsche, the genuine philosopher "lives 'unphilosophically' and 'unwisely,' above all *imprudently* and feels the burden and the duty of a hundred attempts and temptations of life—he *risks* himself constantly."

The Natural History of Morals

Philosophy and the formation of morals go hand in hand, and in *Beyond Good and Evil* Nietzsche provides a "natural history of morals." Although people like to believe that morality follows some absolute truth and is unchangeable, Nietzsche reminds his readers that morals have changed historically along with circumstances and that morality varies from culture to culture.

When reading Nietzsche's thoughts on morality, keep in mind that, in many places, he is making observations (such as the preceding). He describes how *he thinks* morality is and has been created and shaped; he leaves the judgment of that morality to the reader.

In tracing the history of morality, Nietzsche is following his own advice to study topics that are relevant to life. This study also provides another benefit; Nietzsche says that "whoever has traced the history of an individual science finds a clue in its development for understanding the most ancient and common processes of all 'knowledge and cognition.'" This section discusses Nietzsche's history of morals.

Christianity and Morality

One of the main topics in Nietzsche's moral history is Christianity and its systems of morals. Nietzsche writes that "[f]rom the start, the Christian faith is a sacrifice: a sacrifice of all freedom, all pride, all self-confidence of the spirit; at the same time, enslavement and self-mockery, self-mutilation." He talks about the religious neurosis tied to "solitude, fasting, and sexual abstinence" and the "phenomenon of the saint." He offers that others think that saints must "have inside information" because "such an enormity of denial, of anti-nature will not have been desired for nothing."

Nietzsche writes that "fear became rampant in religion" and this fear paved the way for Christianity. He lists still more sacrifices in his "ladder of religious cruelty," noting that religion has gone from requiring the sacrifice of "human beings to one's god" to sacrificing "one's own strongest instincts, one's 'nature.'" He predicts this leads to sacrificing "what is comforting, holy, healing; all hope, all faith in hidden harmony, in future blisses and justices." He asks, "Didn't one have to sacrifice God himself and, from cruelty against oneself, worship the stone, stupidity, gravity, faith, the nothing?"

He talks about how the Church had to "stand all valuations *on their head*" and in doing so they

> break the strong, sickly o'er great hopes, cast suspicion on the joy in beauty, bend everything haughty, manly, conquering, domineering, all the instincts characteristic of the highest and best-turned-out type of "man," into unsureness, agony of conscience, self-destruction—indeed, invert all love of the earthly and of dominion over the earth into hatred of the earth and the earthly.

He contrasts this life-view with that of the Greeks. (This Greek view is closer to what Nietzsche desires.) He says, "What is amazing about the religiosity of the ancient Greeks is the enormous abundance of gratitude it exudes: it is a very noble type of man that confronts nature and life in *this* way." He wonders if the "world-denying" ways of thinking "without really meaning to do so" might have achieved a different goal. They might

> have opened his eyes to the opposite ideal: the ideal of the most high-spirited, alive, and world-affirming human being who has not only come to terms and learned to get along with whatever was and is, but who wants to have *what was* and *is* repeated into all eternity.

Herd Morality

In his description of morality, Nietzsche says the key question is to ask, "What does such a claim tell us about the man who makes it?" He gives some examples of the reasons or purposes, including "to justify their creator before others," "to calm him and lead him to be satisfied with himself," "to crucify himself and humiliate himself," "to wreak revenge," and finally "to vent their power and creative whims on humanity." He sums up that "every morality is . . . a bit of a tyranny against 'nature.'"

In his description of morality, Nietzsche talks about how strengths in individuals are feared and stamped out:

> The highest and strongest drives, when they break out passionately and drive the individual far above the average and the fiats of the herd conscience, wreck the self-confidence of the community, its faith in itself, and it is as if its spine snapped. Hence just these drives are branded and slandered most. High and independent spirituality, the will to stand alone, even a powerful reason are experienced as dangers; everything that elevates an individual above the herd and intimidates the neighbor is henceforth called *evil;* and the fair, modest, submissive, conforming mentality, the *mediocrity* of desires attains moral designations and honors.

He emphasizes that *"Morality in Europe today is herd animal morality."*

Master and Slave

In addition to describing herd morality, Nietzsche also categorizes morality into *"master morality"* and *"slave morality."* Note that Nietzsche's slave and master morality are not a prescription of what should be; instead, they are a description. Nietzsche in revealing these categories wants his readers to see the underlying dynamics and tensions of these two moralities.

In master morality, Nietzsche clarifies that "the opposition of 'good' and *'bad'* means approximately the same as 'noble' and 'contemptible.'" He says that this type of person "feels contempt for the cowardly, the anxious, the petty . . . the suspicious . . . the begging flatterers, above all the liars." This category of man "experiences *itself* as determining values; it does not need approval." Nietzsche further describes him this way:

> The noble human being, too, helps the unfortunate, but not, or almost not, from pity, but prompted by excess of power. The noble human being honors himself as one who is powerful, also as one who has power over himself, who knows how to speak and be silent.

In contrast, "the slave's eye is not favorable to the virtues of the powerful: he is skeptical and suspicious." Nietzsche says that this type of person honors "pity, the complaisant and obliging hand, the warm heart, patience, industry, humility, and friendliness."

Each morality, then, holds in esteem opposite values and thus they are in conflict. Nietzsche describes this tension: "According to slave morality, those who are 'evil' thus inspire fear; according to master morality it is precisely those who are 'good' that inspire, and wish to inspire, fear, while the 'bad' are felt to be contemptible." *Beyond Good and Evil* provides a description of these concepts, and in his next work, *Genealogy of Morals,* Nietzsche elaborates more on these ideas.

Will to Power

Beyond Good and Evil contains Nietzsche's fullest descriptions of "will to power" (with the exception of the work of the same name whose authorship is questioned—see Chapter 2). Rather than the prevailing idea of self-preservation as man's driving force, Nietzsche says it is this will to power:

> Physiologists should think before putting down the instinct at self-preservation as the cardinal instinct of an organic being. A living thing seeks above all to *discharge* its strength—life itself is *will to power;* self-preservation is only one of the indirect and most frequent *results.*

He says that "life itself is *essentially* appropriation, injury, overpowering of what is alien and weaker; suppression, hardness, imposition of one's own forms, incorporation and at least, at its mildest, exploitation." He describes the individual's will and its "strive to grow, spread, seize, become predominant—not from any morality or immorality but because life simply *is* will to power."

He describes the same concept in this passage:

> Suppose, finally, we succeeded in explaining our entire instinctive life as the development and ramification of *one* basic form of the will—namely, of the will to power, as *my* proposition has it; suppose all organic functions could be traced back to this will to power and one could also find in it the solution of the problem of procreation and nourishment—it is *one* problem—then one would have gained the right to determine *all* efficient force univocally as—*will to power.*

Nietzsche relates this will to his study of morality and philosophy, saying that "[p]hilosophy is this tyrannical drive itself, the most spiritual will to power, to the 'creation of the world.'" In his definition of what is noble, Nietzsche explains how the will to power is unique in noble men, the topic of the next section.

Nietzsche's Noble Man

As in other sections, Nietzsche provides descriptions of different types of individuals, contrasting ultimately with the ideal he then describes. In

Beyond Good and Evil, Nietzsche lists the qualities of what he finds noble. He has the opinion some of these qualities are inherited and some cultivated.

Skeptics and Others

As one "bad" example, Nietzsche describes the objective person, saying that "he easily confuses himself with others," "he errs about his own needs," "he forces himself to reflect on his torments in vain," and he has a habit "of meeting every thing and experience half-way, the sunny and impartial hospitality with which he accepts everything that comes his way." In summary, Nietzsche says that this type of man "proves inauthentic, fragile, questionable, and worm-eaten."

He also describes the skeptic as someone who "is frightened all too easily; his conscience is trained to quiver at every No, indeed even at a Yes that is decisive and hard." And he talks about the type of man who does "not wish to be answerable for anything, or blamed for anything, and owing to an inward self-contempt, seek to *lay the blame for themselves somewhere else.*"

In contrast, Nietzsche offers a different kind of skeptic, using Frederick the Great as an example. He says that skepticism can be "the courage and hardness of analysis . . . the tough will to undertake dangerous journeys of exploration and spiritualized North Pole expeditions under desolate and dangerous skies." He praises those who "will not give up their 'responsibility,' their belief in *themselves,*" men with "the ability to stand alone and give an account of themselves."

Greatness of Soul

In contrast to skeptics, Nietzsche describes the noble man; he says what proves the noble man is not actions or "works," but faith. He writes, "[I]t is the *faith* that is decisive here . . . some fundamental certainty that a noble soul has about itself, something that cannot be sought, nor found, nor perhaps lost. *The noble soul has reverence for itself.*"

Part of being noble is enduring suffering and seeing the potential in suffering. Nietzsche writes:

> The discipline of suffering, of *great* suffering . . . has created all enhancements of man so far. That tension of the soul in unhappiness which cultivates its strength, its shudders face to face with great ruin, its inventiveness and courage in enduring, persevering, interpreting, and

exploiting suffering, and whatever has been grated to it of profundity, secret, mask, spirit, cunning, greatness—was it not granted to it through suffering?

The noble man must also "pass through the whole range of human values and value feelings to be *able* to see with many different eyes and consciences." With these experiences, he can then create values. Nietzsche says, "Their 'knowing' is *creating*, their creating is a legislation, their will to truth is—*will to power.*"

Working from Aristotle's discussion of the greatness of the soul, Nietzsche provides his own description:

He shall be greatest who can be loneliest, the most concealed, the most deviant, the human being beyond good and evil, the master of his virtues, he that is overrich in will. Precisely this shall be called *greatness:* being capable of being as manifold as whole, as ample as full.

Lesser Topics and Style Notes

In addition to the key themes, readers will note a few other interesting elements of *Beyond Good and Evil.* Nietzsche provides some breaks in the narrative and changes of pace with a poem and epigrams, for instance, in Part 4: "A man's maturity—consists in having found again the seriousness one had as a child, at play."

What he writes about women can be chauvinistic and critical. The last sections of Part 7 discuss women, as in this example:

But she does not *want* truth: what is truth to a woman? From the beginning, nothing has been more alien, repugnant, and hostile to woman than truth—her great art is the lie, her highest concern is mere appearance and beauty. Let us men confess it: we honor and love precisely *this* art and *this* instinct in woman.

Part 8, "Peoples and Fatherlands," provides Nietzsche's thoughts on Germans as well as Jews, Englishmen and other "good Europeans." Readers can see from this part that Nietzsche was not a Nazi supporter nor anti-Semitic. Nietzsche does include some criticism of Jews, but he turns this same critical eye to others as well.

Nietzsche concludes *Beyond Good and Evil* with a fond look at his ideas:

Alas, what are you after all, my written and painted thoughts! It was not long ago that you were still so colorful, young and malicious, full of thorns and secret spices—you made me sneeze and laugh—and now? You have already taken off your novelty, and some of you are ready, I fear, to become truth; they already look so immortal, so pathetically decent, so dull!

He ends saying, "[N]obody will guess from that how you looked in your morning, you sudden sparks and wonders of my solitude, you my old beloved—*wicked* thoughts."

7 Ecce Homo

> *When I imagine a perfect reader, he always turns into a monster of courage and curiosity; moreover, supple, cunning, cautious; a born adventurer and discoverer.*
>
> —Nietzsche, *Ecce Homo*

Ecce Homo is a unique autobiographical account of Nietzsche's life and work. Freud said about Nietzsche that "he had a more penetrating knowledge of himself than any other man who ever lived or was ever likely to live," and *Ecce Homo* shows Nietzsche's self-awareness about himself and his life. He lived his life according to the ideals he promoted.

Cited as one of the treasures of world literature and a high point for German prose, this work provides Nietzsche's thoughts on his development, his life, all of his writing, and his significance to philosophy and the world.

About Ecce Homo

Nietzsche began writing *Ecce Homo* on October 15, 1888, and finished it on his forty-fourth birthday (November 4, 1888). He had a mental breakdown shortly thereafter—two months after finishing the draft and less than four weeks after the work went to the publisher. From his collapse to his death, his sister, a Nazi supporter, handled much of his care. She appointed herself his biographer and overseer of his work. She often tampered with his writing and promoted his work as she saw fit. After his death, his family decided not to publish any of the works written before his decline (except *Twilight of the Idols,* which was already on its way to publication). *Ecce Homo* was finally published in 1908.

Because of the proximity of his breakdown to this work, some critics do not give *Ecce Homo* the credit it's due, finding elements of madness in the work and, therefore, discounting it entirely. (Nietzsche's sanity and the affect of his health on his work are ongoing debates for scholars. Some scholars maintain that his last several works were colored by his deteriorating mental health.) The work has been ignored, misunderstood, and mistranslated. Like all of Nietzsche's work, *Ecce Homo* must be read carefully and thoroughly (as opposed to reading just selected passages). In doing so, the reader is likely to find excellent insight for understanding Nietzsche.

About the Title and Style

The title *Ecce Homo* is Latin and means "Behold the man"; these are the words Pontius Pilate spoke when he presented Jesus to the crowd calling for his crucifixion. Nietzsche uses the title to stress his humanity, his reality, saying, "Here is *a man.*"

The work includes a preface and four sections with headings such as, "Why I Am So Clever" and "Why I Am a Destiny." Some critics point to these as indications of delusions of grandeur, but given Nietzsche's sense of humor, he most certainly meant them as ironic. Readers should take them with equal measures of jest and seriousness. After all, he does liken himself to Aristotle's definition of a great-souled person: "A person is thought to be great-souled if he claims much and deserves much."

Nietzsche Lives His Ideals

One of the most striking elements of *Ecce Homo* is the observation that Nietzsche lives the ideals he praises. Nietzsche reiterates characteristics and qualities he holds in esteem, and the reader will note these same attributes in Nietzsche's own life.

For instance, one of Nietzsche's themes is a life filled with gratitude and love, what he calls *amor fati* (or "love of fate"). He also upholds the idea of suffering, and instead of complaining about it, Nietzsche says that suffering has the potential to change—improve even—oneself. Nietzsche talks about his many health problems and how they made his life *better.*

In his work, Nietzsche says a noble character does not hold grudges, does not have a negative or pessimistic attitude for life, and does not wish ill of his enemies. Nietzsche affirms his life, suffering and all, and holds true to these qualities.

Nietzsche on Nietzsche

In the opening preface to *Ecce Homo,* Nietzsche talks about his reason for writing the work and provides his assessment of his character. He's prophetic when he writes about being misunderstood. He writes, "[I]t seems indispensable to me to say *who I am* . . . one has neither heard nor even seen me." He stresses, *"Hear me! For I am such and such a person. Above all, do not mistake me for someone else."*

Calling himself "a disciple of the philosopher Dionysus," Nietzsche talks about what he thinks the goal of philosophy should be. He writes, "Philosophy . . . means . . . seeking out everything strange and questionable in existence, everything so far placed under a ban by morality." Nietzsche seeks to tell "the *hidden* history of the philosophers, the psychology of great names." He talks about the courage needed for real philosophy: "Error is *cowardice* . . . Every attainment, every step forward in knowledge *follows* from courage, from hardness against oneself, from cleanliness in relation to oneself. I do not refute ideals, I merely put on gloves before them."

Nietzsche writes about his gratefulness for his life. Despite everything, he writes, "I looked back, I looked forward, and never saw so many good things at once . . . *How could I fail to be grateful to my whole life?*—and so I tell my life to myself."

Of his works, Nietzsche especially praises *Thus Spoke Zarathustra,* perhaps because Zarathustra is Nietzsche. In *Ecce Homo,* Nietzsche uses words from Zarathustra to caution his readers, "Now I bid you lose me and find yourselves."

Why Nietzsche Is So Wise

In the first part, Nietzsche talks a little about his family history and personal suffering caused by his ill health. At age 36, Nietzsche says he was at his low point. He details a few of his problems including migraines, vomiting, eye trouble, and more. He realizes that 36 was the age his father was when he died.

Rather than complain about his lot, however, Nietzsche explains how this suffering gave him a unique perspective. He writes, "Need I say that after all this, in questions of decadence, I am *experienced?*" He also points out the different "perspective of the sick toward *healthier* concepts and values." He says, "I took myself in hand, I made myself healthy again . . . I discovered life anew, including myself; I tasted all the good and even little things, as others cannot easily taste them—I turned my will to health, to *life,* to philosophy."

Nietzsche could have easily sunk into despair and pessimism, but instead he did the opposite: "it was during the years of my lowest vitality that I *ceased* to be a pessimist; the instinct of self-restoration *forbade* me a philosophy of poverty and discouragement."

In addition to talking about the power of suffering to transform, Nietzsche provides other insights about his character. He calls himself "the last *anti-political* German," talks about his freedom from *"ressentiment,"* describes himself as "warlike by nature," and talks about his need for solitude.

Nietzsche stresses the characteristics he defines as noble: overcoming pity, respect for enemies, and honor in conquest, for example. About his own critical attacks, he reminds readers that he attacks only "causes that are victorious," that he stands alone in his attack, never involving allies to share the blame; that he never attacks persons, only what they represent; and that he never attacks because of bitterness from personal quarrels.

Why Nietzsche Is So Clever

In the next section, Nietzsche addresses some of the key issues of his life, in particular his disbelief in God and the influence of Schopenhauer and Wagner.

He doesn't deny God because of some personal affront or life event. Instead, he simply says his nature does not allow him to believe. He writes, "I am too inquisitive, too *questionable,* too exuberant to stand for any gross answer. God is a gross answer." He equates God with the prohibition "you shall think!"

He writes about his independence from Schopenhauer and Wagner. Although he and Wagner no longer were friends—Nietzsche writes that he did not forgive that Wagner "*condescended* to the Germans"—Nietzsche shows the qualities of the noble man when he acknowledges the impact of this friendship:

I must say a word to express my gratitude for what has been by far the most profound and cordial recreation of my life. Beyond a doubt, that was my intimate relationship with Richard Wagner. I'd let go cheap the rest of my life at any price the days of Tribschen—days of trust, cheerfulness, of sublime accidents, of *profound* moments.

Nietzsche relates some of his personal habits—he doesn't drink alcohol, snack between meals, or drink coffee. He talks about the importance of place and climate, cites reading as his recreation, and provides his imperatives of prudence (summed up as "distance; the art of separating without setting against one another; to mix nothing, to 'reconcile' nothing; a tremendous variety that is nevertheless the opposite of chaos"). Offering an explanation of why he includes these details, he explains that these "small things" are more important and more real than the imaginings that "mankind has so far considered seriously." These include "God," "soul," "virtue," "sin," "beyond," "truth," and "eternal life."

Summing up his life, Nietzsche stresses the importance of humor and the spirit of fun. He writes, "I do not know any other way of associating with great tasks than *play*." He shows his overwhelming acceptance of himself and his life, writing, "I do not want in the least that anything should become different than it is; I myself do not want to become different." He reaffirms this "love of fate": "My formula for greatness in a human being is *amor fati:* that one wants nothing to be different, not forward, not backward, not in all eternity. Not merely to bear what is necessary, still less conceal it . . . but *love* it."

Why Nietzsche Writes Such Good Books

In the next section, Nietzsche talks about how his concepts (such as superman) have been misunderstood; he then provides the setting, personal details, and insights about each of his works.

Nietzsche sums up *The Birth of Tragedy* this way:

The two decisive innovations of the book are, first its understanding of the Dionysian phenomenon among the Greeks: for the first time, a psychological analysis of this phenomenon is offered, and it is considered as one root of the whole of Greek art. Secondly, there is the understanding of Socratism: Socrates is recognized for the first time as an instrument of Greek disintegration, as a typical decadent. "Rationality" *against* instinct.

About this work, he claims that he

. . . was the first to see the real opposition: the degenerating instinct that turns against life . . . versus a formula for the highest affirmation, born of fullness, of overfullness, a Yes-saying without reservation, even to suffering, even to guilt, even to everything that is questionable and strange in existence.

Nietzsche explains his thinking behind the title of his next major work, *Human, All-Too-Human.* He writes, "[W]here *you* see ideal things, *I* see what is—human, all-too-human!" This work, he explains, was "the monument of a crisis," written at a time when he says he was alienated from everything that surrounded him. He writes, "I was overcome by *impatience* with myself; I saw that it was high time for me to recall and reflect on myself. All at once, it became clear to me in a terrifying way how much time I had wasted." He adds that "I had not learned anything new that was useful."

He shows how his sickness helped him:

Sickness *detached me slowly:* it spared me any break, any violent and offensive step. . . . My sickness also gave me the right to change all my habits completely; it permitted, it *commanded* me to forget; it bestowed on me the necessity of lying still, of leisure, of waiting and being patient.— But that means thinking.

Readers can see his acceptance of suffering and his use of it when he writes, "Never have I felt happier with myself than in the sickest and most painful periods of my life."

In *The Dawn,* Nietzsche says he began his campaign against morality: "*The Dawn* is a Yes-saying book, deep but bright and gracious." He compares this work to *"gaya scienza" (The Gay Science),* writing that "in almost every sentence profundity and high spirits go tenderly hand in hand." He also says the basic idea of *Thus Spoke Zarathustra* was born when writing *The Gay Science.*

Nietzsche discusses in most detail *Thus Spoke Zarathustra,* citing several passages from it. He compares the time from the book's inception to creation as a pregnancy, joking, "[W]e get eighteen months for the pregnancy. This figure of precisely eighteen months might suggest . . . that I am really a female elephant."

He talks about inspiration, noting "this is *my* experience of inspiration": "One hears, one does not seek; one accepts, one does not ask who gives; like lightning, a thought flashes up, with necessity, without hesitation regarding its form."

He also writes about the joy he felt during this period: "Often one could have seen me dance; in those days I could walk in the mountains for seven or eight hours without a trace of weariness. I slept well, I laughed much— my vigor and patience were perfect."

He connects *Thus Spoke Zarathustra* with his next work *Beyond Good and Evil:* "After the Yes-saying part of my task had been solved, the turn had come for the No-saying, No-*doing* part: the revaluation of our values." He notes that "the eye that had been spoiled by the tremendous need for seeing *far* . . . is here forced to focus on what lies nearest."

After *Beyond Good and Evil*, Nietzsche wrote *Genealogy of Morals.* He provides the inquiries of this book: the birth of Christianity, the psychology of conscience, and "the answer to the question whence the ascetic ideal . . . derives its tremendous *power.*"

In addition to these, Nietzsche also talks about his other works, including his untimely meditations, *Twilight of the Idols* and *The Case of Wagner*.

Why Nietzsche Is a Destiny

The next section concludes the work, and in this section, Nietzsche talks about his fate, his contradiction of all that is accepted, and his negation of standard morality, in particular Christian morality, which he sums up in this passage:

> That one taught men to despise the very first instincts of life; that one mendaciously invented a "soul," a "spirit" to ruin the body; that one taught men to experience the presupposition of life, sexuality, as something unclean; that one looks for the evil principle in what is most profoundly necessary for growth, in *severe* self-love.

He riles against the demand "that all should become 'good human beings,' herd animals, blue-eyed, benevolent, 'beautiful souls,'" saying that this deprives "existence of its *great* character." He goes on, using a profusion of exclamation points to stress his outrage:

> The concept of "God" invented as a counterconcept of life—everything harmful, poisonous, slanderous, the whole hostility unto death against life synthesized in this concept in a gruesome unity! The concept of the "beyond," the "true world" invented in order to devaluate the only world there is—in order to retain no goal, no reason, no task for our earthly reality! The concept of the "soul," the "spirit," finally even the "*immortal* soul," invented in order to despise the body, to make it sick, "holy"; to oppose with a ghastly levity everything that deserves to be taken seriously in life.

The work ends, circling back to his beginning aim, asking, "Have I been understood?"

Further Reading

Nietzsche's Main Works

The Anti-Christ

Beyond Good and Evil

The Birth of Tragedy

The Case of Wagner

Daybreak or *The Dawn*

Ecce Homo

The Gay Science

Genealogy of Morals

Human, All-Too-Human, A Book for Free Spirits

Mixed Opinions and Maxims

Nietzsche Contra Wagner

Thus Spoke Zarathustra

Twilight of the Idols

Untimely Meditations

The Wanderer and His Shadow

The Will to Power

Collections, Biographies, and Critical Works

Gane, Lawrence and Kitty Chan. *Introducing Nietzsche.* Cambridge: Totem Books, 1998.

Hollingdale, R. J., ed. *A Nietzsche Reader.* Harmondsworth: Penguin, 1977.

Kaufmann, Walter, ed. *The Portable Nietzsche.* New York: Penguin Books, 1954.

Kaufmann, Walter, ed. *Basic Writings of Nietzsche.* New York: The Modern Library, 1966.

Solomon, Robert and Kathleen Higgins. *What Nietzsche Really Said.* New York: Schocken Books, 2000.

Steinhart, Eric. *On Nietzsche.* Belmont, CA: Wadsworth, 2000.

Nietzsche Web Sites

Friedrich Nietzsche Society. www.fns.org.uk. — The official Web site for this society, which was founded to promote the study of the life, work, and influence of Friedrich Nietzsche. The Friedrich Nietzsche Society publishes the *Journal of Nietzsche Studies* and holds conferences. Join the society, get information about past and future conferences, and review the journal at this site.

The Nietzsche Channel. www.geocities.com/thenietzsche channel/. — A comprehensive site that includes many of Nietzsche's works online in both English and German. The site also includes a biography, links to other sites, popular quotes, and a forum for discussion.

Nietzsche Chronicle. www.dartmouth.edu/~fnchron/. — Provides a very detailed chronicle of Nietzsche's life and events.

Nietzsche's Labyrinth. www.inquiria.com/nz/. — Includes partial or complete text of many of Nietzsche's works.

General Philosophy

Magee, Bryan. *The Story of Philosophy.* London: Dorling Kindersley, 1998.

EpistemeLinks.com: Philosophy Resources on the Internet. `www.` `epistemelinks.com`. — Includes more than 15,000 categorized links to philosophy resources on the Internet.

Stanford Encyclopedia of Philosophy, edited by Edward N. Zalta. `http://plato.stanford.edu`. — An online version of the *Stanford Encyclopedia of Philosophy* with entries on philosophers, philosophy movements, and philosophical concepts.

Index